THE KEYS

www.**penguin**.co.uk

DJ KHALED
THE KEYS

WITH MARY H. K. CHOI

BANTAM PRESS

LONDON • TORONTO • SYDNEY • AUCKLAND • JOHANNESBURG

TRANSWORLD PUBLISHERS
61–63 Uxbridge Road, London W5 5SA
www.penguin.co.uk

Transworld is part of the Penguin Random House group of companies
whose addresses can be found at global.penguinrandomhouse.com

First published in Great Britain in 2016 by Bantam Press
an imprint of Transworld Publishers

Key illustration on chapter openers by Danny Smythe/Shutterstock
Jacket and page ii photographs by Wolf Ademeit (lion), iStock (key), Shutterstock
(flowers)

Every effort has been made to obtain the necessary permissions with
reference to copyright material, both illustrative and quoted. We apologize
for any omissions in this respect and will be pleased to make the
appropriate acknowledgements in any future edition.

A CIP catalogue record for this book
is available from the British Library.

ISBNs 9780593078372 (hb)
9780593078235 (tpb)

Printed and bound by Printer Trento, Italy

Penguin Random House is committed to a sustainable
future for our business, our readers and our planet. This book
is made from Forest Stewardship Council® certified paper.

1 3 5 7 9 10 8 6 4 2

To my beautiful woman, Nicole,
thank you for your dedication
in keeping me on track for this book
and always inspiring my best

THE KEYS

WALK WITH ME THROUGH THE PATHWAY OF MORE SUCCESS

This is a story about how you can be self-made. As long as you stay out of trouble, learn the business, and dedicate yourself to your hustle, you can accomplish anything. Seriously. When I look at the last year, I almost can't believe the blessings. God is great, and He has truly helped me realize so many of my goals. The pathway of more success hasn't been easy. No one *ever* said it was going to be easy. I had to weather storms and break through barriers, especially since "they" hid the keys from me, and when I say "they," I mean the people who want you to fail. The keys are guiding principles to prosperity. Think of them as commandments that will lead you to success and then more success.

I've said it to you before and I'll say it again: "They"

don't want you to have the keys. So I made sure I got the keys. People always ask me how many keys there are. There are many keys—an infinite number of keys—that will help you formulate a vision for your life and let you know that you're on the right path. And now, in this book, I'm sharing the major keys (and some bonus keys) with you. I love my fans. Fan Luv is everything to me, and without you I know I would be less motivated. It's a special connection—a vibe. And once you get to know me and hear my real story, it will inspire you to go through your own journey and not only succeed but achieve joy. Success can be defined any number of ways, but true joy can be a goal for everyone.

My phrases and my beliefs are real. They are the keys that will help you because they helped me. They're forged from personal experiences all from my perspective, from life lessons that everyone can relate to. Like most of you I didn't grow up rich. I come from a family of immigrants, like so many people in this beautiful country. My parents arrived from Palestine with nothing, and they worked hard—like so many of our parents—to make sure their kids had a better life. So I worked hard. Man, I worked hard. If my story tells you anything, it's that with hard work you can be Steve Jobs, you can be Oprah, you can be

Barack Obama, you can be whoever you want to be, but you got to get there by being yourself.

And the key to more success is that the work never ends. I'm just going to be real with you about that. Success and prosperity don't come fast. Becoming the best is not a product of luck or magic. And getting lucky once doesn't change the rest of your life. It takes dedication, blood, sweat, tears, and some serious hardship. Just don't give up. Never surrender. I may have been up and down over the years but each time the stakes got higher and I made sure to gain a little more ground with each win. The keys will also keep you focused, no matter how many days or weeks in a row you feel down-and-out.

Now, I know that sometimes at the beginning or when the bag is low you have to chase money to survive. This is a time that will truly test your character. You might even have to take a hiatus from your goals to get the bag up and get your finances right, but you have to keep fighting if you want to keep your dreams alive.

I know it looks easy for me to say this. The young world, meaning as in, the next generation, knows I'm having a legendary run. The deals are colossal. The collaborations are epic. But I know exactly where I came from and the hard work it took. It's been ten years of We The Best, ten years since I started my own company. I'm blessed, but a decade is a long time, and I've been in the game for even longer. What I'm saying is that I'm forty and I'm just now on my way. I will never stop.

The other thing I can't stress enough is that the keys are applicable to everyone's lives. Not just artists or music industry people. Everything you see me do and say can be interpreted for any job, any age, and any aspiration. Fan Luv, we're in this together, and together I truly believe we can be great.

I put my best into this book. . . . It's going to get deep. . . . It's going to get very exclusive. . . . I'm going to tell you things that "they" don't want you to know.

But the real first step to walking the pathway to more success is to give thanks to God and give thanks to life, because without God's love and without His blessings, there would be nothing. We're blessed to have our health, our family, hip-hop, and each other. Be thankful every minute of every day for what you have; don't complain. Keep your energy and vibe clean so that other good people want to be around you.

What's so dope about this last year is that I'm making a connection with people who didn't know me before. And even if people did know my music, these same people didn't know anything about my life. Fan Luv has always been amazing, but this new energy is crazy.

The world is showing me love, and the epic thing is that I am just being me. Being able to do what you love without any pretense or filters is a gift—it makes you feel like you have the greatest job in the world. I need you to *overstand* this the way I *overstand* this. Notice how I didn't say *understand*, because I need you to more than understand—I need you to *overstand*. And listen, I'm not done. We're still grinding. We just getting started. I promise you. And We The Best.

"We The Best"

We The Best means exactly what it says. I didn't say I'm the best. That's an important distinction; I said *we*. That means me, Fan Luv, my team, and everybody who's got love and positive energy. Let me ask you this: If somebody came up to you and asked, "Are you the best writer, chef, producer, director?", what would you say? If you don't declare that you're the best, I'm disappointed. You're supposed to say that you're the best writer, chef, producer, or director, because let me tell you, you're the best. You need to own it with confidence and conviction. Say it to yourself first a thousand times, and then say it to other people a thousand more. For real. Is somebody better than you? Nah. We The Best. You have to speak it into existence. You have to speak your success into existence, because absolutely no one else will do it for you.

That's why when I started my first label, I called it We The Best. Were we the best yet? That's up for debate. But did we have the drive and the passion and the necessary dedication to be the best? Without a doubt. Muhammad Ali, rest in peace, said, "I am the greatest, I said that even before I knew I was." Make your life about fulfilling your vision and dream big. I remember when we first opened the door to We The Best Studios. It really didn't match what I had in mind for our home but it had potential. It was run-down, and the carpeting and rooms were all crazy bright colors, so we ripped it all up so that my office could look worthy of a mogul, from the lighting to the Venetian plaster walls. Every day during construction I would pull up an office chair to the site and watch the crew to make sure that everything was ready. I knew the framed magazine covers were coming and the gold plaques and then the platinum plaques. I envisioned it all.

One of my gifts is that I can see the pathway early. If you look at my track record, a lot of the artists that I predicted would do it, did it. I don't look at where you are. I look at where you're headed. You've got to think future to be future. Just ask my friend Future.

When you speak it into existence it will happen. Right now I'm telling everyone that my new aka is Billi. And I'll tell you why. It's because I'm going to be a billionaire, so now I want you to greet me and call me Billi. This way everything will affirm and reaffirm my vision. You got to speak your wins into existence. We The Best means being the best and letting the world know that We The Best. Who? We.

STAY AWAY FROM "THEY"

You hear me saying "Stay away from 'they'" all the time, but who are "they"? I'll tell you: "They" are the enemy. "They" want to keep the keys hidden and block you from the pathway of more success, and "they" want to see you fail. I've seen "they" out there and I've seen their evil. It makes "they" happy when you don't prosper, and "they" laugh at your plans to make yourself better and get ahead. The person who wants to distract you from your studies or your career with their drama? That's a "they." That's a big "they." But here's a major key: As long as you stay away from "they," you will prosper.

People ask me how "they" become that way. I tell them—hate makes you "they." Back in the day I used to just call "they" haters, but I realized after a while that I had to change that word out of necessity. "They" are sneakier than that—"they" take all forms. For some it will be immediately apparent that there's hate in their hearts, but others have a disguise.

There's the type who will do everything in their power to befriend you; "they" will want to hug you and kiss you, meet your family, and become your friend. You've even got the kind who bring you thoughtful presents. But even if a "they" hid their true nature at the beginning, eventually you'll see their evil energy. The "they" vibe is a mess. You know that feeling in your gut when you meet someone who seems off? Young world: Pay close attention to that feeling and trust your instincts. It doesn't matter how new or inexperienced you are, or how influential "they" are, or what "they" have that you don't. Don't get distracted by the gifts and affection and don't ever think a "they" knows what's best for you.

I'm blessed for a lot of reasons. You can see the blessings in my house, my family, my musical garden, and Florida, but an unseen blessing might be one of the most important—my memory. Anyone who's ever worked with me—and that's a lot of people—will tell you the same thing: I remember. I want this to be put in bold in the book in big letters: **I REMEMBER**. Major key.

"They" tried to count me out. "They" told me I couldn't have a house on the ocean, that I couldn't have a garden filled with angels. "They" told me time and time again that whatever my goals were, I couldn't reach them. And I remember it all—twenty years of doubt and hate. If you're reading this and experiencing doubt and hate right now, just remember I've gone through all of it and triumphed. I've had "they" tell me to my face—to my face!—that I wouldn't amount to anything. When I was working at the very bottom, nobody was trying to hear that I was going to be the biggest DJ in Miami and the world. Nobody thought a high school dropout would ever be a record label executive. Even later, when I wanted to make an album, I had so many people tell me I'd lost my mind. "They" all said, "Khaled, you can't have a hip-hop album; you can't rap." But I found a way. Not only that, I make some of the biggest rap records in history.

And now I got the keys. And "they" hate it. "They" hid the keys from me because "they" wanted to end me. "They" didn't want me to learn that if I worked hard and dreamed big, I'd win. This is exactly the lesson that I want to share with you. Don't let "they" ever tell you anything different.

Because "they" are petty. The whole lot are busybodies who want to get in your head and ruin all the pleasure in your life. "They" don't want you to win. "They" don't want you to do 360s on a Jet Ski. "They" don't want you to have stars on the roof of your Rolls-Royce. "They" don't want you to enjoy your best life.

So how do you make sure you do all the things that

"they" don't want you to? Take out the trash. Rid yourself of all the "they." As soon as "they" show you their true colors, act fast and cut them loose. It's like breaking a hit record or making a new announcement—timing is everything. And the time is always now.

I know that when I say take out the trash, it sounds simplistic. Making that choice in your mind is easy; you're a boss, and you do what you have to. But actually deciding to go out and take out the trash can be difficult and requires a lot of follow-through. You just have to remember that "they" will try anything to make you change your mind. "They" will try to confuse you and beg you for another chance, or try to argue and blame someone else for their mistakes.

But when you've got a "they" on your team, you have to move. I can't stress this enough. Don't just talk about that person behind their back or start beef on social media. It's not only a waste of time, it's the first step in how you become a "they." Tell them straight up that "they" are no longer a part of the team and why. Just do it. Don't wait for something to change. Don't start second-guessing yourself. Here's another key: When a "they" is on your team, it's like a cancer on your future success. Think about that. "They" are stealing from your future, the future that you work hard every day to make sure you reach.

Part of making sure that you're keeping trash off your team is keeping a small circle. Now, my circle's always been tight, but as the successes get bigger, I tighten up my circle more. It's very important. I've seen people make mistakes and do the opposite. Some people can't handle success; I can. What that means is that some people sabotage themselves when they're on a winning team. When a boss's circle gets too big, people on the team start thinking they're bosses or make sloppy decisions because they get gassed or greedy. The more people you have around you, the more chances one of them is a "they." "They" are everywhere, so this is just math and logic. Small circles mean you have a better chance of getting all the ungrateful people out of your life. And "they" shouldn't take it personally because it's business. Now, I'm not saying that just because we're hot, we're trying to leave people behind. It's that a certain number of wins can change someone. You've heard it before: Power corrupts.

That said—and this can be sad—sometimes you can have a good friend who turns into a "they." People change. It's human nature to evolve. Now, you can be a good friend and try to help a "they" out and tell them to cleanse off, maybe jump in the ocean—use that salt water to rinse off the evil. And when it's an old friend, you might really go out of your way to try to change them. But let me tell you: Once someone turns into a "they"—even if it's your oldest, closest friend—most of the time there's no changing back. Hate makes you "they." Jealousy makes you "they." And since We The Best, that hate and envy won't stop.

The point is, some people can't elevate their vision because they don't want to progress in the pursuit of prosperity. Instead of being inspired to new heights, they want to drag you down to their level. So just be straight up. Tell them it's time to part ways. It's not just a matter of cutting them off, it's that they're cutting themselves off. It happens all the time. Do it quickly and clearly. I just tell them, "Yo, don't ever walk into my house with any negative energy in your life." I don't care who it is or where we are. If there's a room, I'm out or "they" out. Period. My people know this.

I can't stand ungrateful people. Ungrateful people are some of the evilest "they"s I can imagine. I know some people who are ungrateful to where it's so disappointing, but it's called "Congratulations: You played yourself. Look at us. We're not stopping. So whatever plan you had in your head with your ungratefulness and your complaining and your evil and your doubt, it's not going to work."

Fan Luv is beautiful, and I've got so many fans, but if you know me personally . . . like, if you've been to my house and really know me, you know I always help my family, team, and loved ones, and give back to the community. Some of it you see, or maybe you read about it online, but a lot of it is anonymous. I help people out in so many different ways, so when I know someone who is ungrateful, I have to get them out of my life. It's unfortunate, but lately I don't even waste time thinking about "they." That's not selfish; that's me taking care of my vibe and making sure I stay positive. This is a lesson that really took me a long time to learn. Prioritizing yourself isn't a luxury, it's a necessity.

It's real out there. But you have to believe in your instincts and your vision because when you stay away from "they," there's a reward. There's a feeling out there that the whole world is missing out on, and it's called joy.

Joy is an all-body experience that touches your soul. Some people think they have joy now, and they might be happy, but what I'm talking about is really special. True joy. You're going to be so much better once you stay away from "they." You'll feel like you're living a whole new life, a life free of hate, doubt, envy, and trash vibes, and let me be the one to tell you that *that's* when you can start winning. Major key: The ungrateful and jealous "they"s are the most dangerous "they"s out there.

"They" Don't Want You to . . .

"They" don't want you to have breakfast. "They" don't want you to have Jet Skis. "They" don't want you to have Jay Z as your manager. I don't know if you sense a pattern here but let me tell you: "They" don't want you to have anything worth having. If it brings you joy or success, you can guarantee that these people will do everything in their power to stop you from accomplishing it. You see me on Snapchat or with Fan Luv and you'll know that I'm always talking about all the things that "they" don't want you to have. Stay woke. Constantly remind yourself and speak out loud on the things that you want in life. Picture yourself having everything. It might be a boat, or a plane, or a platinum plaque or a bestselling book or even egg whites, turkey sausage, and a glass of water for breakfast. You deserve all of these things as long as you work hard. Envision all the obstacles you might run into while trying to get them, and then beat them down. " 'They' don't want you to . . ." is like a battle cry against the "they" energy. Go out into the world and declare what you want even if "they" want to stop you. Always do exactly the opposite of what "they" want, and you'll prosper.

I HAVE SEEN Khaled work for years—hustling to put together these songs, get clearances, have people work together that normally wouldn't. I have always been a fan of his work ethic and passion. I love how he never gives up and puts his ego to the side to get the job done. He told me he moved his family to NY to get [my] verse. I wanted him on my team after that! Ha. What we are seeing from Khaled now is really who he is; the cameras are just capturing his natural state. That's why the world is so drawn to him. The most important "key" is honesty: It is best to be a failure with who you are than successful as someone else.

—Jay Z, legendary rapper, CEO of Roc Nation, and Khaled's manager

BE YOURSELF

I'm always telling you to be yourself all the time. I know it may be easier to conform, and it's okay that you might want to follow your friends, but just remember that you don't have to.

I don't know how not to be myself. I told you there was no blueprint for me. I never followed the journeys of any of the types of rappers you saw at the time I was coming up. I wasn't a gangster or a drug dealer, and not to say that you had to be one of those things to make it, but I still hustled every day. A lot of people I grew up around, that was their life, and everybody had their way of hustling and that's what they spoke about. I had my way. But my grind wasn't easy. I would inherit other people's problems and headaches that I had to navigate my way through. Coming up in Miami also made me different. I love Florida more than anything, but I was a big fan of Southern, New York, and West Coast rap. There weren't a lot of people in my hometown at the time who were into what I was. I remember I'd have my friends in New York record radio shows on cassette tape and send them down to me. I used to go to music seminars and DJ battles all the time. I'd always make sure to fly to New York to buy vinyl and to tape Red Alert, Funkmaster Flex, and Clark Kent on the radio. I'd go watch and study Kid Capri at the clubs because his mic game and his selection were unbelievable.

But being unique in Miami ended up being a huge blessing. Often there was no one else in my lane. We didn't have mainstream hip-hop radio stations in Miami, so I made that work for me.

When I was working at a pirate radio station called

Mixx 96, it was just me playing that kind of stuff, so I owned that whole market. When you're an original, you'll look crazy at first—and let me be honest: you might look crazy for a while—but eventually people will know exactly what to come to you for.

Having a distinct brand and voice helps you corner the market. I've always had that big personality that loves connecting people and making people smile. But sometimes being yourself isn't easy.

I love hip-hop and genuinely think there are a lot of geniuses in the culture who I'm blessed to work with, but over the years there have been occasions when people mistook my kindness for weakness. I have a big heart and I promote peace and unity, but sometimes that's not the most popular way to be. Hip-hop can get real sometimes. People think beefs sell a lot of records, but they're wrong, and that's why I stay out of it. My character can be seen as the opposite of all that. I believe in my vision, and I can't be any other way. People might think loving peace is soft, but we all know that's not true. It takes all the strength and discipline in the world to stay calm in certain situations. And I won't lie, there have been times that I had to remind people of my power just in case they forgot and mistook me for someone they wanted to test.

It's the strongest, wisest man who knows how to come to the table seeking solutions.

It doesn't matter what everybody else is doing; I just have to keep doing me. Even if it's unpopular or people don't understand it. Because when you ain't yourself, how are you living with yourself? Think about that. If the person you are when nobody's watching is so different from who people *think* you are, how is that not a waste of energy and emotion? I know some people who have like three or four versions of themselves, and I don't honestly know how they keep track. How can you claim to have a focused vision when your head is so mixed up?

Who does your team even know to follow? You can't keep the pathway to more success clean if you don't even know who to be. Meaning as in, be yourself.

Being yourself means first learning who you are. Take time to identify and develop your natural talents and you will be successful. Also, take time to figure out what makes you happy. If you combine what comes naturally to you with what makes you happy, then you will be unstoppable.

Also think about the parts of yourself that you get from your parents—who they are and the way they raised you—and the parts that you learned from the teachers in your life. I don't just mean at school; I mean wherever you worship, in the streets, from your mentors. Add these things to your talents so that you become better at your passions. Don't just be a star, be a superstar.

The other part of being yourself is also being true to what makes you unhappy. I despise "they." I can't stand liars and disloyalty and complaints. I keep these things out of my life at all costs. Removing what makes you unhappy will make you happy. That sounds obvious, too, but believe me, people forget to take out the trash all the time.

Being yourself is power. In some ways, of all the major keys, it's the most important key. But it's the hardest to master. It's the one you have to keep working at as life goes on, and it's the one that leads to the others. Not being true to yourself is how you know that "they" are in your head. That's real talk. Ignoring who you are will eat at you. When you live life by what you think other people want from you, you aren't really living. Over time it might make you feel hollow or hateful.

Because here's a major key: Know that most people in the world aren't being themselves. Being real when other people are fake is what sets you apart. The issue is that it's easy to forget who you are. Especially if you're young. Especially if you're different from everybody else. People are suspicious of people who stick out. But there's no path to more success where the first chapter isn't being yourself. Matter fact, look at any artist or successful person. I guarantee that there isn't a single person I look up to who wasn't called crazy or weird at some point in their life. "They" will always tell you that your ideas are stupid and that they're never going to work—until they do. This is the hardest part of being yourself; it's risky. It's scary to think that people might reject you or what you create. There's nothing to hide behind, and there's no one else to blame. But you have to be fearless. No one else is going to ride for you harder than you will. And being loved for being someone else is an empty life. You'll never experience true joy, and a life without true joy is not living. Once you learn who you are and the rewards come, think about how to be better. It's not about changing the essence of your personality and character; it's about working on the parts of you that may not be the best yet. This is how to become more than who you're born as. This is how experience and wisdom make you develop into a better person, and this is how your goals get bigger and your standards get higher.

Maybe it's learning to become more patient. Or spending time with your family. I try to dedicate time to enjoying life now. And I'm working on my health and anxiety.

Just understand that it all takes time. The journey starts with making peace with who you are, accepting that you're one of one, and loving yourself so other people can, too. Then give thanks and make sure to live well by making yourself better *your* way.

"Special Cloth"

I've always been special cloth and I've always known. Knowing I was different is one of my earliest memories. Think about it: My first and last names are the same; I'm Khaled Khaled. From the beginning I dealt with kids telling me that I was a liar, and it's not easy to argue with everyone about something as fundamental as your own name. See, "they" were after me even back then. This was even before I knew to call them "they." Being special cloth makes "they" show themselves early.

Special cloth. What does that mean? It means that you're special edition. You're one of one. Like they broke the mold after you. Matter fact, there wasn't even a mold, because you're a masterpiece. It means that when people compare you to everyone else, it doesn't make any sense.

From a young age I knew that I was blessed by God. I am God's son. It's called always knowing that I wanted to be the best. It's called knowing that I was different from everyone else. Everything I do is Khaled. I don't even have to try; I can't help it. It's a special thing. We love Barack Obama, Muhammad Ali, Jay Z, Michael Jackson, Michael Jordan, and Martin Luther King Jr. because these are all special cloths. Prince was special cloth. Rest in peace.

When you're special cloth, it's hard at first. There are a lot of challenges because it can be lonely. People try to confuse you and try to change you, but when you keep working and putting your unique brand out there, you find out there's other special cloth in the world. That can be a huge relief. Matter fact, sometimes you can bring your specialness together, collaborate, and make something amazing. That's what I do.

There was no blueprint for me. You can just tell by knowing me that I'm one of one. Some people might call it passionate. Other people call it annoying or loud. I don't care what "they" say. The important thing is just to block out the negativity. Just make sure that your cloth is the finest cloth. Keep studying what makes you happy. Keep grinding and getting better. Learn everything you can and stay hungry. Study the business and the moguls who came before you. If you meet another special cloth, learn about what makes them special and *overstand* more. You might be born special cloth, but don't take it for granted. Oprah, now, she's special cloth. We look up to Oprah and we're inspired, but go read her story; it didn't just happen. Oprah had to make sure she became Oprah. Remember that. Make sure that you become the you you're meant to be.

KHALED IS A hard worker, he's dedicated and focused. Khaled's show came on after ours and I don't remember exactly what building we were in, but we were on a high floor and he would come and start bringing in equipment all by himself, like one crate, two crates, three crates . . . MPC, turntables, and I just remember thinking, "Just how many trips in the elevator is this man taking?" He would do this every time, and the second we'd finish he'd start setting up his stuff. He was never late, never skipped a beat. I'll never forget me and Dre ended up leaving for Atlanta for some R&B endeavors and we were gone for a while, and we gave Khaled our six-to-ten slot, which was prime time, because he used to go on at ten p.m. to one in the morning. And when we came back everything was DJ Khaled.

We stayed close because we haven't fallen into the music industry crap—the bullshit that comes along with the music business. Sometimes you might not be popping or people might be saying shit or people didn't get on certain projects that you got on and feel some type of way, but we never fell into any of that with Khaled. Khaled doesn't operate like that. It's always been a mutual respect with him. Any time something came across the table for us to speak highly of Khaled, we would do it, and whenever something came for us, Khaled would speak highly of us. We're just grateful to do business. We all work so hard on our own visions and have so much love and respect for each other. We produced his first single and the majority of the first album, so it's been a special relationship since the beginning.

He was the first one to buy his house in our area, and then me and Dre went and bought houses right after, and when he had the pool put in and we were swimming in the Jacuzzi, it was so hot you could have boiled some eggs in there, and he's like, "Cool, we did it, we did it!" I'm like, "Khaled, how do you even have skin left, bro? This shit is blazin'." But he had the Jacuzzi cranked up because "they" didn't want him to have a Jacuzzi. He's a great example of what happens when you follow your dreams and stay the course. If there's something out there that you really believe in, do it. Stay focused and stay away from "they." Be original and don't stop. Everything he's done, it's because he believes in himself, and that's how me and Dre have gotten to do everything we've done. Don't count on nobody else, and once you have that vision, it's damn near impossible for you not to win.

—*Cool, producer*

WE MET KHALED at an underground radio station in 1996. We were just fresh out of high school, and Cool and I had been producing and making beats as kids and trying to get on. We were like seventeen and he was like nineteen. We really were kids. We had a little time slot on a mix show, and back in the day in Miami you really couldn't get the music you wanted to hear; they weren't playing New York or West Coast hip-hop. You'd hear the hits like LL Cool J but we didn't have a mix show like a real DJ playing the dope shit that the streets were tuned into. You would get more pop-rap, which there's nothing wrong with, but the way the local radio was doing their shit was what gave someone like a DJ Khaled the space to come and occupy it. Cool and I were on the radio station; it's illegal and pirate, it would move around. We'd be good for a couple months in this building in North Miami and then it'd be like, "Oh shit," and we'd have to move it over here in the hood now. When we met Khal, his approach was just honest. He said, "Yo, check this out, I'm new. I just moved here from Orlando and I'm trying to get time on the radio and 'they' be hating." So me and Cool immediately were like, "No problem," and the minute we said that, the man walked in with so many crates of records, a beat machine, a recorder; he was just prepared for us to say yes. This man came with a production. Our first impression was a lasting impression. He was about his business. Cool and I left to pursue our careers as music producers and we were even singing in a group at the time. And we stopped doing our radio show and Khaled got our time slot, and we were in Atlanta chasing L.A. Reid, trying to get down and to see if he'd sign us. We made some headway but after nine or ten months we got back to Miami and the guy that we met, the new guy, he owned the city. He owned Miami. It was the wildest shit. In nine months he took over Miami. Everybody was tuned into what DJ Khaled was doing on that radio. It's the same energy but a younger version, it was really uncut. If you think Khaled's uncut now, I dare you to meet a twenty-year-old Khaled. That's my earliest memory but that just showed us that he was a force to be reckoned with. We actually saw it from the beginning, from when he first moved to Miami and we watched him become one of the hottest people in the city, period. He's a hell of a DJ and he's sick and he knows how to blend his shit, but the energy that he puts behind the music, that's his gift. He took over Miami quick and all the clubs he would DJ at, you just had to be there.

And the thing is, Khaled's loyal, too. We had a meeting with Fat Joe at Hit Factory, and he was the biggest artist besides maybe Juvenile at the time. So this was a huge deal, and Khaled walks into the session and was like to Joe, "Oh shit! This is who you got the beat from? These are my brothers." He just walks in and stamps us and gives us that cosign of trust. Joe could see how happy Khaled was about it and he trusted Khaled, so he immediately took us in as family after that. Khaled's seen me and Cool's progression from the birth, and we were there for his as well. We have a lot of special moments over the last half of our lives that we've shared with him. That's special and unique. Khaled is also just a very driven dude. When he has his eyes on a goal he's gonna get it. And we don't have regular goals, we have the loftiest of goals. That's what he means when he says, " 'They' don't want you to have that." I remember when I bought my first Bentley. One day Khaled just gave me a talk. I was good at the time, I was driving a Benz and I had a Range, but Khaled pulled up to me at a hotel in a brand-new GT coupe. Nobody had it and I was like, "Wow, Khaled, that's how you're doing?" And he goes, "Now you've got to get it." And I said, "Nah, I'm good." And he goes, "No, Dre, 'they' don't want you to have a Bentley so you've got to make sure you get it." And this was 2006. It's amazing to be able to see how this same personality, the guy that he's been, is so influential and infectious. We always knew it—we know his influence on the circle and what it's like to be in the studio with him because he inspires you to be great—but now everybody gets to see it and read about it, and it's beautiful.

—*Dre, producer*

DON'T
EVER PLAY
YOURSELF

Major key: Don't play yourself. What I mean by that is don't do anything foolish to compromise your joy and prosperity. People play themselves in a variety of creative ways. Maybe their ego gets the best of them and they brag about having something when they don't. Or else they violate the code and try to lie about it. If you're someone who laughed at me and doubted me—that's one surefire way to play yourself. For real. I hope I don't need to spell out all the ways that you can play yourself, especially if you're of a certain age and level of experience, but if you're young and new, let me be clear: Just because you play yourself once doesn't mean they can count you out forever. Just never make that mistake again.

Playing yourself becomes a cycle. Play yourself once and often you'll find yourself playing yourself over and over in an effort to dig yourself out. That's called turning a bad situation into a worse one. You're turning a tiny speed bump into a serious roadblock.

When I was a kid, sixteen or seventeen years old, I used to get into a lot of trouble with my driving. I used to get pulled over every day because I had a suspended driver's license. This was when I had a little career going on in Orlando. Me, aka Beat Novacane; DJ Nasty; and DJ Caesar had just founded Hitmen Productions, and we were all making music, throwing parties, handing out flyers, and selling mix tapes. This was back when they were actual cassette tapes, too, so I'd sell them out of my car. To be honest I just thought I was doing my job and being responsible by earning steady money the best way I knew how. And you know how young people are; when it came to my livelihood you couldn't tell me nothing.

Now, if you know anything about me, you'll know I'm relentless. When people tell me no, it just makes me go harder. Back when I was young I was even more hard-headed, and the way I saw it, I didn't make these rules; they seemed arbitrary, so neglecting them didn't seem like the worst idea.

Besides, this was Florida. The thing about this state is that back then you could get stacks and stacks of tickets. You'd pay your $75, you'd get points on your license, but that was that. A ticket was a minor offense and everybody treated it as such. In any case, I had this lawyer who would always get me out of everything. He was a family friend, and since selling mix tapes and spreading a love of hip-hop felt like a victimless crime, I didn't think it was a big deal.

This was the drill: They'd run my plates, pull me over, make me go to court, I'd go to court, and after listening to a speech and paying my fine and getting my points, I'd get off. When you're young you really think this can go on forever. It doesn't occur to you that it might snowball into a different type of situation.

But of course it eventually caught up to me because I didn't learn from my mistakes on my own. One day it had gotten so bad that the judge had had it. I walked in that morning thinking I was going to get out in a few hours but she made me go to jail. Just like that. She was like, "I'm tired of seeing you in court. I'm tired of you not learning your lesson. Your lawyer isn't going to save you this time." Looking back at it now, I realize that it was bound to happen, but that's the thing about being a kid—you're just not convinced of the consequences until you have to face them. But boy, that day I got the message. All of a sudden the cops came behind me and cuffed my hands behind my back. That was it, I was arrested, and it felt crazy because it was the last thing I expected.

Of course my mother and my father lost it. What mother wants her son getting locked up? They were just as surprised as I was, and I was shocked. But that was it—I had to go. Eventually I got out but it was enough. I'm not saying that my experience of going to jail for what was a very small period compares to what other people have to go through. Our prison system is flawed and unjust and the realities of that are heartbreaking, but what I can tell you is that for me, one time was enough. We see prison on TV or in movies, but when you're inside . . . All I'm going to say is that that place is not for humans. Places like that will strip anyone of all humanity. I will never forget that, not ever.

What I'm saying is that I may not have caught on quick enough to avoid jail, but that one time became all the lesson I needed. I didn't know I was playing myself, but that was what it was. I know it doesn't sound like anything that deep or dark, and it happened a long, long time ago, but the reason I bring this up now is because I want the young world to know that jail is not for them. Getting locked up, no matter how long, is not for you. And because the system is rigged, once you go in, they do everything in their power to make sure you go back. I don't want anybody to have to experience that, ever. Fan Luv, keep your face clean and stay out of trouble. Please.

Now that I had that memory, it definitely stopped me from making that mistake again. And it changed how I made decisions. Now I consider the consequences of my actions and even go so far as to think about the worst-case scenario. This one experience made me appreciate that a lot of bad decisions and shortcuts aren't for me. I thank God for this wisdom. If you do play yourself, your mind better click fast and you better straighten up quick. How you deal with this setback will determine the course of your future.

Don't keep playing yourself. Admit your mistake and then don't let them end you just because you're not perfect. Don't think that just because you went through trials and tribulations and you're still growing, you can't be the best. That's a major key.

I know the young world might not want to move with someone else's rules; I told you, I've been there. But it costs money to buy water. I say this all the time. It costs money to have AC, just as it costs money to jump on a plane or drive a car to see your mother. Gas costs money, and it costs money to eat food. When you go to a restaurant, they bring a bill. When you go to a grocery store, same deal. I'm not talking about buying Lamborghinis or jewelry or super-yachts or limited-edition sneakers. I'm talking about the fundamentals—the shit you need to survive. It can be frustrating that there are so many rules for acquiring even the most basic level of what you want, but you just have to push through and know when to neglect those rules and when to follow them.

Here's the other part of the lesson that I want to leave you with. The reason that making a mistake back then was such a gift is that it made me think about the next chapter of my life. I had time to picture what I wanted my journey to be. If I didn't want to get the same result and get locked up again, I had to change my behavior. It's like what they say about the definition of insanity: Expecting a different result from the same actions is crazy. At the time I felt like I was gaining traction with my professional life. I was practicing making beats every day, and these all-age parties we were throwing would actually make money since we'd sell soda for like five bucks a pop, but I couldn't do any of that during this time. I love hip-hop so much, and to think I wasted any time away from my dream over something so stupid killed me. The day after I got out, I moved from Orlando to Miami. I just had to. It was like a big switch just got flipped on in my head.

That night I packed up my records—and it was a lot of records. I had less than $20 in my pocket, just like my dad did when he moved to America, and I had the clothes on my back. I left my parents and my brother and sister and all my friends. Nasty and Caesar would have to drive to come see me, but I just knew that I had to get to the next step of my vision. It was time for me to conquer Miami. I didn't know exactly how I was going to do it, but I knew I had to. And I knew to never make a mistake like that ever again.

"'They' Kick You When You're Down; 'They' Wanna Kick It with You When You're Up"

Sometimes when you soldier through hardship, you've got to keep your head up and just be grateful. Times of struggle might test you but in them, God is also testing everybody around you. Your family, your brothers and sisters, and the people who really ride for you and have love for you will pass that test.

Everybody else will fail. They're "they." It's the best silver lining you could hope for. Everybody has a time when they're down. This is the exact moment that "they" will kick you. "They" are so foolish that "they" just assume it's over for you because "they" see you stressed out. That's cool, though. Matter fact, it's fantastic. Just take a look around and start remembering names and faces.

See who's got your back, and start taking attendance of who's on your side. What everybody else don't know is that while "they" are just wasting their time kicking you and relishing your failure, you're not even focused on being down. You're already figuring out how to overcome the roadblock and how not to be down the next time the situation happens. Plus, you're digging yourself up and rising again.

Suddenly, "they" see that you've got the best logos next to your logo. It feels sudden to them because "they" don't know that you've been planning and focused this whole time. The biggest artists and directors and companies and moguls want to be in business with you, so suddenly "they" really want to kick it with you. It's hilarious to me how these people want to be your best friend when you're up. This can be at work, in school, anywhere. It's a glorious thing to behold, so when you're down just remember that this moment will come. Just watch and smile. That's what I mean by " 'They' kick you when you're down but 'they' want to kick it with you when you're up."

I REMEMBER WHEN I met Khaled, he was still a kid. I was a few years older than him and I came to his parents' store at the mall. This was back when everybody was going there to get their suits made, like, basketball players in the Orlando Magic. I walked in and he immediately starts trying to sell me these pants. I hold them up and I'm a thin guy and these pants were huge, but he kept on like, "No, you don't understand, we have the best tailors. We can custom-fit these for you and they're going to be amazing." I was like, "Nah." But I'll never forget how he's always been such a salesman, even from the time he was young.

Khaled's always had that type of talk game. Like, "Yo, come to this party, it'll be crazy, man." He doesn't just hand out a flyer, he sells a party. He'll strike up a whole conversation with you while he's handing it out. When we were doing teen parties we were handing them out in downtown Orlando, International Drive, we would hit high schools—you name it, we hit it up. Back in the day there wasn't social media so we had to be out there so people would know what was going on. I've known him a long, long time but I can't imagine a single time when he didn't get something that he set out to get.

We have a lot of memories. I remember us DJing

a Biggie concert. It was Biggie, Craig Mack, and they came to Orlando in our younger Hitmen days. Shaquille O'Neal was in the back with us and a fight broke out in the middle of a Biggie set. All I know is that we're huddled up, me, Shaq, and Khaled, trying to figure out how the hell we were getting out of this shit, because all we hear is, "Pop! Pop! Pop!" We were like, "What is that?" Come to find out it was Heineken bottles flying everywhere that were being thrown. It was wild, because just how Biggie says, "Party and bullshit," that's exactly what happened. That's exactly when the fights broke out. It was crazy.

Me and Khaled have just seen so much. Orlando was a melting pot. Everyone from New York would move there to get away from any trouble. These were our friends and these were people who influenced us. We'd be going to Tony Touch parties and we'd get that New York flavor and we'd get the Southern from Magic Mike—these were pioneers in Orlando in the early times. Tony's parents moved to Orlando and he finished up high school so he was there for a year or two throwing parties all over the city. We heard the music he was playing and that was a big deal to us. He was an icon. Me and Khaled grew up listening to all regions but New York was very influential to us. Pete Rock, Brand Nubian, CL Smooth, Gang Starr, that was what we were playing back in the days. We weren't introduced to Southern music until Luke. But that was a little further in. We were playing Big Daddy Kane, Biz Markie, Eric B. & Rakim, and eventually we were introduced to Southern music and Miami bass. That was huge in Florida.

We were lucky to be around one of the huge names of Miami bass—DJ Magic Mike. We would always be hanging out with him. Khaled would play dominoes with him and we'd just listen to music. It was good times.

When Khaled went to Miami that's when he got into Jamaica a lot but he first fell in love with reggae at Dolly's One Stop in Orlando. Dolly was the guy's name. Khaled visited him about a year ago. That's another thing about Khaled, he don't forget. Those people who helped him along the way and were genuine to him, he always tries to see how they're doing and check in and visit. It's always about family. But there's so many reasons I can't see another DJ Khaled. DJs try to do what he's done, but there's only one. Come on, man, other DJs can't do this. Not on the level that he does.

—DJ Nasty, Power 95.3, producer, manager,
and founder of Nasty Beatmakers

SECURE THE BAG

When I say, "Secure the bag," that means don't play yourself before the wire hits. Fiscal responsibility might be the last key you'd expect from me, but it's important to learn if you ever want to be a mogul. Don't do anything foolish before those numbers hit your bank account. People will have the opportunity to get the biggest wire to take care of their families, but they'll play themselves before the funds hit and they can't secure the bag, so they lose the opportunity.

Secure your bag at all times. Get in that zone where you'd rather have money than spend it. Because sometimes when you secure the bag, then you can secure a bigger bag just because you have your paper at the right place at the right time. It's about having a down payment for the next investment. This is what I mean when I say the answer is always more success. It's called having enough cash to buy into the bigger deal.

I got to go on the road all the time. Do you think I want

to leave my musical garden? Do you think I want to leave my angels? But I got to work hard to keep the garden and maintain my dream house. I know I'm blessed. I got a pool and a Jacuzzi and I can buy my girl the flashiest car on the road, but if you know us you know that before we buy anything I have to make sure I'm straight. You've seen me on Snapchat asking my management team, "Did the wire hit yet?" I ask all the time. Don't be embarrassed talking about your own money. Securing the bag means knowing where your money is at all stages and all times.

But that's not all I mean by "secure the bag." It's a metaphor for success and opportunities. When you play yourself in front of a boss, that's called not securing the bag. When you study hard for ten years to become a doctor but you get drunk and act crazy the night before your final test and fail, that's called not securing the bag. Being reliant on other people's money is not securing the bag. You want to be independent? Secure the bag.

I learned about securing the bag from a young age. My parents always supported me, and they always wanted me to be happy. My family are all hard workers, and that's where I get my work ethic from. I saw my parents sell clothes out of the trunk of their car on the street and at flea markets because I would go with them to help. For years I would talk to customers and organize inventory.

When we started I was a little, little kid—maybe seven, eight, nine. And then my parents owned a shop in a strip mall, and after a while, from working hard, they made it to where we had a store called Park Avenue in the Florida Mall.

All of this, seeing what my mom and dad had to go through, was inspiring to me. They both have great business minds, but even more than that, they worked hard. They worked twenty-four hours a day, seven days a week. My father and mother had no sleep for years. It's why I don't ever make excuses. Matter fact, I hate excuses. It's an insult to hard workers. I remember I used to work at the store behind the counter. We had the best tailors, and our specialty was high-end suits, and we would suit up NBA players on the Orlando Magic like Shaquille O'Neal. We were well-known throughout the city, and a number of other celebrities used to support and love our shop.

But "they" didn't want my family to prosper. One day we had it all—a successful store, a house, a car—but the next day it was all gone. Now, this is a story I don't like talking about or even thinking about, but when I was young—barely old enough to drive—I was out one night working. I was working a party and right in the middle I saw that someone was calling me from the phone in my home studio. This confused me for two reasons: one, because it was late for anyone in my family to be calling, and two, because the only person who ever went in there was me. I picked up and heard my mother scream before the line went dead.

You can imagine the thoughts running through my mind as I raced home to find flashing lights and police swarming my house. I rushed in to make sure my parents were all right, and thank God they were, but they'd been roughed up and robbed. They'd tied up my father and mother and sister and taken everything. My mother, being the brave woman that she is, tried to lock herself in my studio to call me before they found her and cut the phone lines.

At this point I was still just a young man, but I was old enough to feel a mixture of fear and rage and whatever the emotion is when the most important people in your life are threatened with violence. My mind was so overcome with thoughts of vengeance, and as I prayed to God for strength and wisdom, in my heart I just hoped that I didn't know the people behind the home invasion. I prayed that I wouldn't lay eyes on the people responsible and recognize them, because I knew that when the time came I would do everything in my power to destroy them.

I know that this chapter began with the most literal

definition of securing the bag—money—but nothing about me or the keys is literal. Securing the bag sometimes means not ruining your future. Now that I'm older and wiser I know that I have too much to lose to exact revenge, but back then? Back then I don't know what would have happened. In those days I was just starting my business and was really from the street when it came to my reputation, and it's by the grace of God that the police caught the robbers and they were strangers.

Unfortunately, this wasn't the only hardship my family would endure. Almost immediately after they lost everything in their home, my parents ran into some financial trouble with the business. These two events combined finished them, and a few years later they declared that they wanted to leave Orlando. It was a dark time. They packed up and wanted to move in with some family in New Orleans to get back on their feet.

At the time my music career was blossoming, and since I had been spared having to take revenge and was old enough to secure my own bag, I decided to stay. Florida was my home and I had big plans to eventually move to Miami, but I also didn't want to be a burden while they got their bag up. So they went one way and I went another.

I said good-bye to my family, to my parents who I love

so much, and became determined to become so prosperous, so successful, that I would one day be able to help them. I was focused. I'd just broken some barriers with "they." I was throwing my own parties—things were popping—and "they" had just started to let me DJ in the club. I was even being invited into the studio by a few local artists to play some of my beats. This was big for me; we were still at the ground level, but I could see where it was going because it was the start of my vision. I told my parents of the plan, they gave me their blessing, and from there I got an apartment.

Getting an apartment was easy. Keeping it was hard. At the time I was making like $100 a week with two jobs and whatever else I needed to do to make ends meet. I was just a kid and I got evicted probably ten times; you know how it goes when the bag is low. You pay one month and then you ain't paying again for like two, three months. "They" start coming after you, and "they" want you out, so you go. Trust me, what young world goes through to make rent, I went through all that. My friends would come over and I would have no furniture. Nothing in my fridge. Just records. Records were my furniture and the floor was my bed when I went to sleep at night.

Every day I would get up and raise money to get another place to live. Those days were rough, and it was real hard to work through it, and at a certain point I couldn't find another apartment. That was it. The bag was beyond low. The bag was, like, negative.

During this time I ended up going to New Orleans to live with my parents. I've lived in Florida most of my life. This is my home, so it broke my heart to have to leave. But what I'm saying is that I went back because it got so rough with money that I had to stay at my mom and dad's house. It hurt my pride and was a source of great frustration that I was depending on them when they needed to figure their situation out.

I only went back for a year, but I had to work for that year so I could return to my home. There was no choice. I lived with my parents and started working at a Shoney's as a busboy and at a record store called Odyssey Records & Tapes.

I hated being away, but I knew I had to secure the bag. I put my head down and just saved all my little checks from the jobs. But knowing what I did about being on my own, losing my apartments, and not having enough money to eat, I didn't get comfortable sleeping at my parents' house. I didn't spend anything. I knew I had to secure the bag, so I saved. And then God really blessed me. There was a DJ contest. I'd been practicing all the time at the record store, where I'd set up some turntables, and I knew I could do it.

When I was up there just tearing it down, I was so determined to win. My energy is already crazy, but on top of that I had a fire because I had a goal—I had to get home to Florida and I had to become a help to my parents, not a burden. I was just in that zone where after you're done you maybe don't even really remember what happened, but when I looked into the crowd I knew I'd ripped it.

I won five grand at that DJ contest. The opportunity was such a blessing, and it came at exactly the right time. Over one year I secured the bag, saving up my $200, $300 weekly paychecks, but that five grand put me over the top. It was what I needed so I could rent a little U-Haul for all my records and drive back to Florida.

I got another apartment and started it all back up. I took a one-year break to get my money right, but it was worth it. I had to secure the bag to come back to my vision and my dream, but there wasn't a day in New Orleans that I got confused. I knew the minute I could go back to the dream, I would do it.

"Don't Complain"

Complaints are excuses, and excuses are for the weak-minded. People who have long-winded explanations about why they can't do things never become bosses. That's just a fact.

Nobody's going to follow this kind of negativity into battle because complainers waste the day imagining new bad scenarios and spend no time accomplishing the vision. People like this can be so creative when it comes to new ways to be frustrated and annoying. Whenever I wake up and I just don't feel right or I feel down, I do everything in my power to change it. I don't want to be a "they" today. That's how it starts. Why spend all that time and energy focusing so hard on roadblocks and then telling everybody around you how life is hard? Of course life is hard. Nobody said it was going to be easy, and I guarantee you that someone else has it harder. If you'd rather make excuses than succeed, be my guest. Complain your annoying little heart out. Just don't do it anywhere around me.

KHALED'S SUCCESS IS *no accident. He never let any lock, any door, or any roadblock block his dreams. His knowledge is firsthand and invaluable for all aspiring hustlers making their dreams come true. The Keys* *shares his journey and it teaches us all how to follow our own path to success.*

—Sean "Diddy" Combs, recording artist, actor, designer, philanthropist, and CEO and founder of Bad Boy Worldwide Entertainment Group

LIFE IS WHAT YOU MAKE IT, SO LET'S MAKE IT

Life is unpredictable. I look at some of the things that happened to me over the past twenty years, and I gotta be honest with you: It's like a movie, for real.

You already know that negativity is not the answer,

but you've got to go the extra step—be positive. Just as there are a lot of storms to endure, there are also moments of pure joy. Recognize these for what they are and be open to them, because sometimes blessings surprise you at exactly the right time.

I've always been one of those people who look at the positive. Now, that doesn't mean that I'm naïve or that I allow people to take advantage of me. It's just that most situations are a matter of perspective. It's why my friends' blessings make me happy, not jealous, regardless of how I'm doing. And when I'm down, I just think about what I can do to get up. There's no sense in just being depressed about it.

Different stages always signal different struggles, and there was a time in my life when things were really looking up. You have to understand that I started throwing parties when I was young. Me, Nasty, and Caesar started Hitmen Productions when I was, like, fifteen or sixteen, and we hit the ground running—our parties always did well financially. And we'd throw them once every few weeks or months.

When we started out in Orlando, we threw house parties, but then we moved our operations to a spot called the Lebanese Club on the corner of Mill and Colonial. It was official. We'd have security, a girl in the front taking tickets. There would be like a thousand people, and it would be poppin'. We'd charge $5 for a cover, and we'd sell sodas, so that was a nice hustle. That was enough to where it was a job. We could make actual money doing what we love: DJing, listening to hip-hop, and catching a vibe with our friends. After that I finally got to move to Miami and started working the nightclubs there, DJing and tearing it up. I loved that my dream was coming to fruition in a city that instantly felt like my home.

But dark days did come. That year in New Orleans was tough. I'm not going to lie to you; leaving my friends and my hustle and my dream was hard. But it was something I had to do at the time so I tried to stay positive, even though I hated being away from home more than anything.

During the time in Louisiana I worked at a record store because I've always loved them. Back in the days before the Internet, me and Nasty would get all competitive about who would get the white-label promo records. I used to make sure to develop relationships with all the little mom-and-pop record stores so that they'd give them to me first. Even though me and Nasty were in the same crew, that was just how we'd get a little competitive, because getting one of those promo records was so rare and we both loved the challenge.

I set up some turntables behind the counter at Odyssey Records, where I worked, so I could practice and make sure I kept all my skills up. That was like my little office, too; sometimes when the boss wasn't looking, I'd make some long-distance calls to different people in the industry, trying to hustle and network. Anyway, people would walk in and I'd be mixing it up and scratching while they bought CDs and tapes. Birdman used to come twice a week with Slim, his brother and partner in Cash Money. I'll never forget—they would bring me CDs and tapes to stock out of their trunk. We'd talk, and I just knew that he was special cloth even back then, and I swear every time they came in and dropped off music, it didn't matter how many it was, they'd sell out. Always. This was before social media, so it's not like it was on Twitter or something that they brought new music in. It didn't matter when they brought it in; an hour later, it'd be gone.

Birdman and Slim were always grinding, and just seeing them and their focus inspired me. They were doing their thing in their hometown, and watching them made me hustle harder so I could get back to Florida. It gave me hope for my own dreams. And then, months later, to see them get a huge record deal at Universal was all the motivation I needed. Back then, in the late nineties, that contract was huge. Hundreds of millions, and they got to own their own work. It was crazy. Matter fact, I even saw Birdman meet Lil Wayne for the first time in that store. That's historical. You never know when history's being made all around you. Even though I was down at the time, this gave me hope, knowing that it was all possible. So I spent this time focusing on my vision and my long-term goals. This is when I pictured my dream house, my garden, the career that I wanted, and my best life.

Life is not a game, but what we do is joyful. Making music is a pleasure, and it's a blessing. I am so grateful that this thing that I love so much can pay my bills. That's why you've got to stay positive. You can't approach someone already thinking they're going to say no. They catch that negative vibe, and it makes them feel like you're a negative person. Wake up each morning and expect the best to happen to you that day. No matter how dark your yesterday was. That's what I mean by "Life is what you make it." Make your life great.

I KNEW A long time ago that this guy was special. I met Khaled a while ago at a convention and we'd hung out in Miami and he always said he was going to take over the radio. Next thing I know, we're back in Miami and we turn on the radio and it's like Mobb Deep, Fat Joe, and I'm like, "Oh shit, Miami came up," because they never used to play real hip-hop. Then the guy on the radio comes on like, "This is Don God Gargamel, this is DJ Khaled, Terror Squad!" He's going crazy on the radio and I'm like, "Oh shit, it's Khaled!" It's me, Big Pun, and a couple of other fellas in the car and then we're like, "Let's call him up," so we write the number down. We call him, he gives us the address, so me and Pun go and just started freestyling and rapping on the underground radio station for like two hours. Callers are clapping and the three of us, shirts off, sweating bullets, no AC, we were wilding out. We just had a real serious bond with him.

Plus, he wouldn't stop harassing me. Every time it would be like, "I want to make an album, I want to make an album, I want to make an album." I knew he had the potential to do what he wanted and he wouldn't stop, like, "I'm the biggest shit, I'm the biggest shit!" telling me I had to put him on. I told my friend Alan Grunblatt, who first signed me, that Khaled was going to be big. I told him he was me on steroids. So he ended up working with Khaled and that was the best decision he ever made. That's what I love about Khaled, just that energy. We've always loved him. Pun used to even drive down to Miami just to play him records. Khaled was the first one to hear "Twinz" and even then he tried to steal it from us so he could play it first. We were like, "Hell no, Khaled, stop." Khaled can't stop. It's one of his best qualities.

—Fat Joe, rapper and CEO of
Terror Squad Entertainment

WEATHER THE STORM

They never said weathering the storm was easy. It's going to rain some. It's always going to rain some.

You notice how I started off this book talking about the pathway to *more* success? I say *more* to imply that the pathway is long. There are ups and downs. One success is fine, but as I've said before, We The Best—one blessing is not enough. You could be enjoying the brightest moment—the sun is shining on your face, you got a raise or a promotion—but that storm could be lurking just around the corner. It doesn't matter who you are. You could be a CEO or working in the mail room; there will always be storms.

But just as storms come, storms also end. The key is to keep your head up and work through it with your mind focused. Life is like school; you will be tested. The key is to pass it. And you have to do well on those tests over time in order to graduate.

Success is a process.

Dark days are challenging, but they're important. Struggles help you know. Once one storm tests you, the next time you know to get food and water, usher your pets indoors, and protect your windows at the first sign of a hurricane. The following time you might have enough wisdom to get gas or a generator. Time after that you could be such a pro at weathering storms that you've secured a safe place stocked with absolutely everything you need where you can take other people in and protect them. Living in Miami, we know storms. Most of the time it's beautiful. Not even a hint of a cloud in the sky, with a balmy breeze, and everyone is just out swimming, laughing, wearing sunglasses, and chilling. But when the storms come they change everything. At this point in my life I can smell the electricity in the air and see how the light moves low before it gets dark. These days I can see most storms coming, but even I have been surprised.

I've been living in Miami now for a long time and I knew from the moment I arrived that I wanted to make this my home. I bleed for Miami. I wave the flag for all of Florida but I love Miami like no other. But that doesn't mean it's always been easy. I told you when I got locked up I drove out here right after. I also told you about the hardships I had to endure trying to secure the bag, but those storms didn't stop. When I first moved to Miami permanently, it was in a black Honda Civic with my girl-friend whose parents lived here. They were divorced and her mother would let me sleep on the floor in her house, but when my girlfriend was at her father's house I had to sleep in the car. Her dad didn't want to allow another man in the house, and I respected that. Sleeping in my car was a huge storm. No bathroom, no showers—that was hum-bling. And that was a time I couldn't prepare for simply because I was just getting by to survive, but I'm grateful for those dark days because they made me hungry. Every morning that I woke up even more tired than when I went to sleep, sweating like crazy because I didn't have any AC, I knew I didn't want to sleep in a car ever again.

But just because I had to weather a hard time doesn't mean I got down about it. Self-pity was a luxury that I couldn't afford. Every day was a new opportunity to get out of my current situation. I had to find a new oppor-tunity, and thank God that this was the time I met the people at Mixx 96. (I would love to name names but since it was pirate radio, I gotta respect the code if you know what I mean.) I will always be grateful they showed love.

I met Cool & Dre at Mixx 96. These are my brothers, and I had the show after theirs. From the moment they said I could be part of the operation I always made sure I was prepared. I had all my crates with me and was never late. It didn't matter if it took me thirty minutes and like seven trips to the car to get all my records in the hallway; I was always the most professional, and then I'd tear it up. Some nights I even slept in that station, and though it got hot in that little room, too, it was a lot better than the car. Not having a place to sleep gave me perspective and taught me gratitude. That's what I mean when I say storms are important. After that Cool & Dre went to Atlanta to pursue their dream of becoming producers and gave me their time slot. It was still a crazy challenging time but with each small step up, I knew the storm would end.

The thing is, when I look back at my life I wouldn't trade any storm in my path if I had to do it over again. Every time I had to struggle, I learned how to avoid it the next time or how to get out of it faster. It's called experience. I have a big heart—anyone who knows me can testify to that—and I try to help anyone, anytime. Because I've seen so many different types of challenges over the course of the last twenty years I make sure to help people weather storms. I might help people even though I'm in a storm, too. Because there were definitely times when I was struggling that people saw my hardship and thought to help me out.

All storms end. And when they do, you'd better make

sure you know who helped you. This is a major key. Those early days at Mixx 96 might have been a struggle but people definitely looked out for me, like Joe Crack, my brother. He lived in New York but would always visit a lot. And even though we were a small operation at Mixx 96 we were killing it, and he really believed in everything I was doing. It meant so much to me that at the top of his game he and Pun would cosign me to be a part of Terror Squad and show me love. People wouldn't even believe that I knew them and then they'd come to the station, where it was small and hot, and freestyle for hours and take calls. You have to understand, this is like a dream come true as a fan. I've seen Pun record, and that's a legendary experience and a blessing that I'll never forget. Joe lives in Miami now, so you know that all of the relationships and outlets I have here, from radio to the club, I always make sure to show love right back. There isn't a version of a Khaled story that could be written without Joe being in it. And that's what I mean by letting the people who embraced you and showed love during a storm know that their help did not go unnoticed.

Hardships also help you focus. Even when I got more successful and way later when I finally had enough saved up to start this business, there were moments when I had to sacrifice my mortgage to pay my studio bill. To me, these were days when I needed a studio more than I needed a home. I'm the guy who always had a state-of-the-art studio before I had furniture or paint on the walls in my house, so this will come as a surprise to no one, but these decisions were tough.

In the end I made sure to hold on to both, but I knew that I needed the studio for my future. I needed it to record the anthems and I had to have an office for me and for my team. It was a turbulent time but I knew I had to risk my house to get to the next level. I just really, really didn't want to go back to sleeping in my car, and I'd been scarred by seeing my parents lose their home, but I had to bet on me and face the storm.

Here's the other thing about storms: As you get bigger, they get bigger. The tests get harder as you get smarter. This is when the key is to have all the keys—start thinking about how all these keys fit together. Think about patience, think about "they," think about your backup plans, and think about your vision. It will help you.

The other thing to remember about challenges is that you must always expect them. You are one person on this gigantic planet; there ain't no way a storm won't come for you if it wants to come for you. It doesn't matter if it's been a long time since you had a storm, or if you just had a storm. Man, I've had storms within storms. Some seasons they just come. Be humble, know it can happen, and make all the arrangements so you can get through it.

The only part of any of this that you can even hope to control is to always give your best. No matter if you're up or down, no matter if your war chest is empty or you're tired. Never surrender. Embrace the blessings, but sometimes it will be more important to embrace the storms. Because storms keep you humble. In turn, humility is what makes life sweet. As I always say: It's not an easy road, but give thanks to the road. You will never be happier than when you know a storm is over. When you're on the other side and the sun is smiling on your face and your yard is green from the rain and your angels are happy and there's a rainbow on the water, you will know joy. Storms are what make every win sweeter.

MY INITIAL IMPRESSION of Khaled was hearing him on the air in Miami at WEDR. At the time he had just become an artist, but he was still a fixture on that radio station. And we were in the process of putting a radio station on to compete against his.

Much to my surprise, he was quite friendly and receptive to establishing a relationship. And since we played his music, he gave us equal access to the music as he did his home station. I just thought he was a really nice guy.

He was—as he is now—extremely charismatic, and the relationship blossomed. He's always been the person that whenever he promised he would do something, he's done it. And I can't be mad at anybody that keeps his word the way he does.

He came across at a time where people began to give attention to producers à la Quincy Jones, you know, but without a doubt, Khaled being the most charismatic of them all. It's hard not to like Khaled. Khaled is just a teddy bear, you know? He's just a nice guy. Beyoncé was here in town this weekend and it was hard to get a ticket; you know, he got me tickets, which was kind enough, but he just went above and beyond, like made sure I got to my seats properly, sent out one of his people to check on me. It's just Khaled, he's always been that way. There've been times when I've run into him in a nightclub in Miami and he was just always, "Hey, come sit with me, I take care of Doc! This is Doc!" It's difficult for me to think that anybody could have a true beef with him.

And then he just got into this Snapchat thing that has just become absolutely insane. I could be on the front page of any magazine and not hear a word, but when I'm on Khaled's Snapchat, I get people all over the world saying, "My God! I saw you on Khaled's Snapchat! Oh my God!"

—*Doc Wynter, director of*
Urban Programming, iHeartRadio

"THEY" GONNA TRY TO CLOSE THE DOOR ON YOU; JUST OPEN IT

We all experience doors in our lives. And by "doors" I mean obstacles. No matter how high you climb the mountain, there's always another one after it. And sometimes that next mountain is like Mount Everest—it's huge. But you've got to keep going and breaking through. I always say: They gonna try to close the door on you; just open it. If you can't open it, break it down, rip the door off, and put them hinges in the haters' hands. Sometimes I use a word that's stronger than *haters*, depending on the vibe, but this is a book, so I'm gonna keep it professional. Now, when I say *break* and *rip* and all that, I'm not promoting the use of violence. Please don't ever get confused.

First of all, we only break the door down when we have to. We don't break the door down for fun. Only crazy people with too much time and anger problems break the door down for fun. This is about necessary force. This is for survival. This is for when we don't want anybody to stop our blessing. We need our blessings. Not only that, we like our blessings. I told you "they" tried to close the door on me all the time because "they" didn't see me coming. There was no road map for me. Who else came up the way I did? At every stage, for every win and every blessing, "they" said no. Every time, I had to turn no into yes. There are times to be humble and follow rules, just like there are times to rip down doors. The key is to know the difference.

When you first get on, it shouldn't matter what type of business it is—take the opportunity. Get through that first door—just open it. Meaning, at least get in the building. It might be that the first situation won't make you rich or famous. The first step is often an internship or a few years spent as an assistant. That's okay. People are impatient sometimes, and they think they're too good to start at the bottom. That's playing yourself in a big way. That's called having a short-term vision, aka the wrong vision. The key is those first opportunities lead to more opportunities.

For me Mixx 96 was that first shot. That was my first radio experience and a great place to learn because there was so much freedom. That's the blessing of a pirate radio show and that's what I mean by taking full advantage once you open the first door. Once you're in, keep your eyes open. You smart. You *very* smart. But even if you're smart, learning the business could take a minute. Ask questions to the bosses who will make time for you and move with a clean heart, aka do good business, aka respect the code. Of course you're going to come across people who don't appreciate your greatness, and any business is rough because you can be fooled in the beginning or people won't see your vision—but push through. Remember these early days and think about what kind of boss you're going to be in the future. Know from the mistakes they make.

When you're special cloth, a lot of the time people don't understand you. In order to really be happy you have to be yourself first, and if you're one of one, people get confused. They want to put you into a box or put limits on you, so make sure your vision is so huge that it destroys the box and those limits. This is you getting to that next door. You've got to let everybody know that there's no door that can keep you out. Those doors might be expectations or people saying no. The key is to know that a no isn't a death sentence. Get through that door and change their minds.

After Mixx 96 I had the incredible opportunity to work with one of Miami's most important icons—Uncle Luke. That's Luke Skywalker; he's a Florida legend, so when he called me after I was killing it on underground radio, I was honored. I'm always going to be grateful to Luke for that. He said he wanted me to be his cohost and his DJ at 99 Jamz—that's the big radio station, WEDR, in Miami. It was the Friday night show, the hottest show in the city, and it was so live that crowds would gather outside the station when we aired. It was a vibe. After a while Luke would go on tour so I ended up getting my own show, and from there I got a mix show, which led to my own night show, which was number one for over fifteen years. But just because I found my way into the mainstream didn't mean there weren't doors. At first when I wanted my own night show the bosses said no. Straight up. They weren't trying to hear it. But when I see a door like that I just get into a mode where I can't accept the answer. I just kept asking.

When you get into that zone people might think you're crazy. And they might find you frustrating. They're like, "Who is this guy who's just not going away?" Then something changes. This no-saying person starts to get a little curious about why you want to get through so damned bad. They might start asking you questions and find out what you're about. Then they actually start respecting the hustle. When you're out there putting in work and they see it every day, your determination is undeniable. Let me tell you, after twenty years of business and friendship, these people who said no become your brothers. It happens.

But other times you will need to destroy that door. This is the second part of the key. If you can't open it, break it down. Rip the door off and put them hinges in the haters' hands. You put them hinges in their hands so "they" can remember. So "they'll" know what happened and there's no confusion. If it's a "they" that's keeping you out, you've got to do what you've got to do—you've got to go through them.

If you paid your dues, mastered the game, stayed respectful, and worked hard to where your knowledge is undeniable, make it your mission to destroy that door. Get up earlier, stay up later, keep your mind clear, and do it.

You can say no to me a thousand times, but I'm still going to keep coming. I am single-minded in my pursuit. I don't get embarrassed or mad or feel disrespected by the process. To me, it's a simple difference of opinion. You can't see my vision. I get that, but I will do everything in my power to try to convince you.

I could see my special chemistry with the audience. I'd experienced it with the crowd and I knew that they wanted me to have a show—not only at the turntables but Monday through Friday night as a personality. So after a while I turned it into a campaign. It was like running for president. People at the radio, like all the people who worked there, started wearing T-shirts like "Khaled for the Night Show!" and it became a movement. When I eventually got that show I knew it was the best situation for everyone. Think about it: Me ripping down that door turned into a beautiful career and a number one show that lasted for over fifteen years. That's how wrong people can be when they first tell you no. That's why you can't listen to them and why you can't quit.

For real, sometimes, when they finally say yes and you walk through the door, the person on the other side might change your life. From those early years to now this has always proven true. I will never forget how it took me a whole year to get a Jay Z verse a few years ago, but now he's my manager. It's unbelievable but that's a fact. Now we're building the vision together. Plus, I have even more Jay Z verses. God is good and the wins are sweet. "They" don't want me to be the biggest DJ or the biggest producer in hip-hop. "They" don't want me to break the most legendary new acts this culture has ever seen on my label. Just like "they" don't want me to celebrate the ten-year anniversary of We The Best with more major successes. But look at me—I'm doing it all. And this is why I'm sharing the keys with you. So you don't have to break down every door, but some of the time that's what it takes. And for each of the doors I broke down, I had to be patient. Some doors take years to break down. I don't break down doors because I'm in a rush; I feel like that gets misunderstood sometimes. I've got Fan Luv and major magazine covers, but when people call me an overnight success I laugh.

But even while you're patient, just hustling and grinding at your vision, you've got to be thinking about the next door. Matter fact, you got to keep your mind on a few doors. That's why when I was younger, while I was doing the radio show and working my way up, I was still thinking about producing. After a while I had a vision to make a mix tape, so I made a mix tape, then I took everything I learned and wanted to make an album. The album was a huge door. I had to look up at it, it was so enormous, and the whole time people thought I was crazy.

These days people might think that all the doors are ripped down in my life. Doors are never going to miraculously just open for you. I think what's going on now is that the whole world is seeing my hard work at the same time. Snapchat opened some doors, but now there are bigger doors. I only ever wanted to be in music, but now I also want to be the biggest mogul. I want to make movies, television shows, and more books; I want it all. My love of music got me everything I want and I'm looking forward to getting more. And I know that means more doors, but I'm ready.

IN KHALED I see some of the same qualities I saw in Jay when I joined Roc-A-Fella Records in 1996, which makes twenty years this year. Leadership, limitless creativity, and an ambition that is unmatchable. When Khaled talks it can come off as unrealistic, until he accomplishes exactly what he says he'll do. He always gets his win. We met through music but it's his relationships that really make him special. This man's relationships are unheard of. People know they can trust him. They want to be in business with him and they love him. Besides, he stays making hits, so what's there to lose?

—*Lenny Santiago, senior VP of Roc Nation*

STAY HUMBLE

I'm humble. I was born humble, but now I get humbler every day. Now, just because I'm humble doesn't mean I'm not confident. I'm bold and I know I'm one of the greatest to ever do it. I'm an icon, and I let the world know it, but being humble means being grateful for your blessings and remembering everyone who helped guide you to them.

Right now is a special time in my life. I thank God because of the level of blessings I have the opportunity to experience. Every time there's a new deal alert or a new announcement, I'm humbled. How could I be anything but humble? Please just look at the reality of my life: I toured with Beyoncé and President Barack Obama asked me to personally talk to him about young world at the White House. I'm on a level of grateful that I can't even properly articulate. It's amazing.

You have to understand, I'm a fan of this music and culture for real. I remember from the time I was thirteen years old daydreaming about all of this and setting goals. I would sit in a garage, covered in wall-to-wall posters of Run DMC and KRS-One and Eric B. & Rakim, plotting and scheming about how I was going to make an impact in this world and culture that I love so much. And now at forty I'm seeing these dreams being realized. When I'm shooting a video in the Bahamas with Nas, you have to believe I've been thinking of this moment from years before. That's Nas! I had a poster of him on my wall when I was growing up. You can feel my joy because I'm just so happy I can't believe it. I get to do my favorite thing—make music—with icons. That's humbling.

This is why I don't understand people who are jaded or don't appreciate their role in the most incredible industry in the world. And of course this is a deeply personal experience and goes for any industry. Depending on who you are, being a fashion designer, or a chef, or a director might be the most amazing thing. I will never understand people who work their whole lives to win, and then when they do, they try to act like they're already over it. Don't ever play yourself.

I fell in love with the culture during a great time—an iconic time—when I was super young. I remember listening to NWA, Public Enemy, EPMD, A Tribe Called Quest, Leaders of The New School, and LL Cool J. Then, after all that greatness, you've got Nas, Jay Z, Biggie, Tupac . . . the list goes on. It's a privilege to play a part in keeping that going. Being around greatness from a young age made me aspire to greatness, but that's also why I'm so grateful. I always give credit where it's due, and part of giving credit is studying the game. Learn every name that means something to the people in that business. And when you have the opportunity to meet these people, appreciate their greatness and show gratitude. Now, they might not be famous or a household name, but these people are all visionaries who can teach you something.

Knowing the pioneers of the game—whatever your game is—is unbelievably important. You've got to know who put in the work ahead of you for you to be able to do what you're doing now. It's one of the best ways to be more inspired about what you create. Listen to their stories, and it will help you write your own. If you're a fan of the music and the people responsible for it, you'll discover that you see your own music differently. If it's sports, memorize the lessons of the legends. Whether it's the process of making a hit record or being a star athlete, figure out how they work. Figure out the connections. Take someone like Lyor Cohen, who's a great friend of mine. He is not an artist himself, but this is a man who's worked with Jay Z; he's worked with everyone from Run DMC to Whodini, Kurtis Blow to the Beastie Boys, Slick Rick to Bon Jovi, Method Man to Mariah Carey.

Not only is he a major part of history, he's still a part of the story, which is a testament to his greatness. He's been a chairman for years, from Def Jam/PolyGram/Universal to Warner Music, and now he has his own new company, 300, through Google and Atlantic Records. If you want a break in music and you have the tremendous luck to run into Lyor Cohen, you better know exactly who he is.

Once you know the history, you're more invested, and that keeps you humbled and excited. I keep loving hip-hop and I love the new artists. They might not be new-new, but they are undoubtedly the faces of the next generation. I'm talking about Future, Nicki Minaj, J. Cole, Drake, and

Kendrick Lamar. I like to know what's going on, and I pay attention because I don't want to miss out. Having that drive is also a part of being humble in a way that will only serve your career, because new energy can be very inspiring.

There's nothing like watching a young artist just tear it up in the studio; their expression when they're in the zone and they know in their mind that they've got a hit is amazing. Or seeing them get excited when they meet their heroes; that's a good reminder of why we do this.

If you start getting a crazy ego about how hot you are, you might not have the opportunity to take part in the next generation. That's some dinosaur shit. You've always got to be looking out for who's next, who's hot. You never know when you're dealing with an artist who might give you that holy grail.

On my album I have a track with Jay Z and Future, "I Got the Keys," and it's unforgettable, but what I will always remember is when Jay did "They Don't Love You No More" for my eighth album, *I Changed a Lot*. That was a huge door I had to open. I really needed something special. I needed that verse—that blessing from Jigga—to elevate everything to the next level. Jay Z is timeless, you can't deny his greatness, his voice and his verses are forever. That's what I love about him. He's a mogul. At this point in his career he doesn't have to make music. But he does it for the culture and his love of the game.

But of course Jay doesn't just give you a verse. It takes a whole lot more than just asking the man. You know I had to get on my tour bus and move my girl and my business operations to New York for a year straight just to get that verse. I stayed focused; I didn't get mad and I didn't get frustrated. What's there to be frustrated about? Jay Z doesn't need to give me a verse, so I've got to convince him to give me a verse. I stayed humble and showed him I was relentless, and at the end of the day our relationship and his being my friend made it happen. Every morning I woke up and I believed I'd get that verse. Sometimes you want to give up—I just don't.

It was amazing when it finally happened. I knew my energy had paid off. We were in the studio recording several times, and then he finished it on the road. And it was such a blessing, because, man, that's a new Jay Z verse in the world. That's exciting. I'm a fan first, and that's huge.

"Catch a Vibe"

When I say "Vibe with me," it means "Let's chill and have a good time." When everybody's in a positive mood and everybody's just having a good time, that's called catching a vibe. Everyone who comes to my home knows about the vibe. Look in my fridge: There are delicious juices and smoothies. I have healthy snacks all over my house for everyone, the chef will cook up whatever you want, and you can sit by the fire drinking Cîroc or D'Ussé or some Belaire and relax.

People who have love for me need to feel welcome. It's hard out there in the world, so when people are near me, I want them to be comfortable. I remember when I started throwing my birthday party; it's called Temple, and it's been going on for fifteen years. Temple is all about getting a religious experience through music. But the best part is that I got to bring acts down to Miami from everywhere—Busta Rhymes, Trick Daddy, Rick Ross, Fat Joe, Pun, M.O.P., O.C., Canibus, Wyclef, Puff Daddy, Swizz Beatz. From Kanye West to Lil Wayne and Birdman—too many artists to even name here, but just everybody would come and hang out. At the beginning I would DJ, but now it's like a concert but in a party style. It's to where I can't even tell you who's going to perform because people just go off. It's a celebration. You'd think it was like the Grammys or the BET Awards, because everybody comes. Just all the private jets flying in.

These artists were in Miami, so to me it was like they were in my home. In the early days I would even pick some of them up from the airport, but no matter how big the party got it was always all love because I made sure it was that way. They knew that when they were tearing it up with Khaled it was a special situation. So when I say "Catch a vibe," it's always the most positive vibe. It doesn't matter if it's just a few people over at my house or thousands of people in the club; I keep that special energy around me. It makes people want to be around you and want to work with you, too. Good energy attracts good energy, so make sure your vibe is the best.

KHALED USED TO DJ at my club on South Beach at a party called Rockers Island. It started in 1996 and every three to four years we changed the venue but it's still going on today twenty years later, the same event on a Friday night. He was a hip-hop DJ and this was a predominantly reggae party. He wanted to play hip-hop and at first I told him no. But he would push and ask over and over and then he started playing and scratching and pulling all these tricks and the crowd went wild. Khaled's work ethic is one of the things that I most admire about him. This man does not take no for an answer. People say that a lot but you don't really understand until you meet DJ Khaled what that means. When you tell Khaled that you can't do something or something's not happening he just doesn't hear you. It's amazing because he gets everything done that way. It's been something that I've taken on in my own life and business since meeting him. That whole approach works.

The Khaled that everyone sees now has the same energy as he did when I met him in 1996. Nothing changed. This is really who he is. To this day if he needs something from you right now, if he's like, "I need you to pick me up at the airport," he's not going to stop if you don't answer about picking him up at the airport. It's as simple as that. The guy is persistent, and it's an amazing characteristic because it really does work. Talk to anyone he's ever worked with and they'll tell you the same. He has to be persistent chasing artists, chasing lawyers. His path hasn't been easy.

I have this story about Khaled that I tell all my staff members who are new to the organization, and it goes back to loyalty and being careful in the industry that we're in. Be mindful of the money that we generate in that your loyalty has to be bigger and a lot stronger. I consider everyone I work with to be a family member, and Khaled worked with us for about two to three years. When Rockers Island got shut down at Amnesia, Khaled was working with me every Friday making money. But the owner sold the building so we were out of a venue, and it was hard for me to find another one. Maybe on the third or the fourth week he called me at the house and told me he'd gotten a call from another nightclub to DJ. He really needed the money. He said, "My mortgage is due, my car note is due, and I don't have any money but I'm going to stay with you." That floored me, because he had a choice to continue his own life and get back on his feet instead of waiting with me to get my situation together. And not only did he say that, he did it. I realized that this was a special guy, because anyone else would think about themselves first before another person. He could have lost so much but he waited. I will never forget that.

—*Joey Budafuco, event promoter*

RESPECT THE CODE

Respect the code. It's that simple. Treat people the way you want to be treated, keep your word, be trustworthy, stay loyal, and don't be evil. Do all these things together and you will have the best relationships. People are envious of my relationships. Let me tell you, God is good but it's not a miracle that allows me to do business with these amazing, inspiring people. It's all in the way I respect the code. These are people who rely on me personally and as a business partner and people I rely on in return. I'm blessed to call them my friends.

Having that understanding—that trust—is important if you want to accomplish big things. The code isn't mysterious; it's not a hidden key. It's just that a lot of people are shady and petty and love wasting energy trying to ignore the code. If you spend too much time with people who deny the code—and these people are definitely "they"—you might think it's natural to promise one thing and then deliver another. You might think it's okay to make deals to get ahead and not make good on any of them. If you do that you will fall. And let me tell you, fake friends don't care when you're down. That's just obvious.

Special cloth are unique and sensitive. Brilliant minds can't work until they trust you. The geniuses I work with know that not only will I grind harder than anyone else in the world to make a track shine, whatever happens in the studio stays in the studio. There's no drama and bullshit when we work. It's all love and good energy.

The code is about respect. If you want to be respected, respect has to be earned, and the first step is that you've got to respect that person, too. If there's a phone call you got to make before you make a move, do it. If you're about to do a deal with someone your friend doesn't like, let them know. Tell them it's not personal and all parties will respect you for being up-front. They might not enjoy what you're about to do, but they'll appreciate you for your honesty. I'm always on the up-and-up because I work with big people. You have to be. Big people don't get big by not respecting the code. Especially the types of people I make money with. I have love and respect for everybody and ultimately my relationships are everything to me. I refuse money because of my relationships, because that's also the code. I refuse money all the time.

Now, I'm not the type of person to tell people exactly

what I do or don't do. I don't have to tell my partners every time I refuse money, but let me tell you: The people who know *know*. I never have to mention it. That's the code. Bosses know, and they remember. Most of my relationships I've had for a long time. Jay Z, Joey Crack, Rick Ross, Puff—these men are like brothers to me.

But I understand that when you're coming up, it's hard to say no to a quick deal. I won't lie to you; the temptation is real. But let me be clear: Respect the code even when it's hard—especially when it's hard.

For me, in my early Miami days, I knew I had to build my name and my reputation. Those were some challenging times. In those days, I didn't always have a place to live; that's just what it was. At the time I wanted to DJ in the club so bad, but I knew that I had to prove myself. There was this guy, Joey Budafuco, who everybody called "Budda," and he was this big important guy when it came to the Miami party scene. He was a big man who stood around six foot five, and I'll be honest with you, he might be my family now but back then he was a little intimidating. Budafuco threw this incredible party called Rockers Island in Miami and I would ask him all the time to let me DJ. They played reggae and some hip-hop, and I knew that if I got in there it would be amazing. But I also knew that I had to respect the code and prove myself. So for a while I just handed out flyers and even worked security for VIPs whenever he needed me.

It's not that Budafuco didn't want me on, but he didn't really know who I was yet. At the time I was hosting the pirate radio show but knew I had to figure out a way to get to DJ in the club. It was just a matter of time. He needed to see what I was about, so I worked and waited and was just always around in case that opportunity came. I stayed grateful and didn't complain. I played my position. So one day, and I don't even know why, he turned to me like, "You know what? I'm gonna let you DJ a fifteen-minute set." Now, you know I'm always ready, so of course I had my records with me and it was on. Major key: Always be prepared for the next step in your vision. I tore that club up so legendarily, and everyone was happy for me that I killed it. After that every Friday was my night, and it became the hottest party.

Everything was incredible but there came a time when Budafuco's party lost its venue for a few weeks. And of course it just so happened that it was exactly the time when I had bills due. As I was wondering how I was going to pay everyone, I was approached by a competing club to DJ for a quick check. I had a decision to make, and it shouldn't surprise anyone that I decided to respect the code. My reputation is everything. So is loyalty. Budda looked out for me when I needed him to, and these are actions I will never forget. I told Budafuco I was going to wait for him, and after a few Fridays we were up and running again. We weathered the storm together, and after that, business was booming and our bond was unbreakable.

When everybody respects the code and moves with a clean heart, everybody thrives. When I say I'll do something, I do it. That's my word. When I say I'll help you, I'll help you. When I say you're going to have a good time at the most legendary party, that's a promise. And in case you forgot, I keep my promises.

"Bless Up!"

When I was young I fell in love with Rastafarian culture. And that love only grew over the years when I started going to Jamaica. Hip-hop was my first love, but I love reggae and dancehall. Mavado is on my label; Buju Banton, Stephen Marley, Rohan Marley, Bounty Killer, Capleton, and Elephant Man—these are my friends. You'll hear Sizzla playing in the background of my Snapchats, and you'll notice I always play conscious music in my musical garden. *Bless up* comes from this culture. It might be the way you greet somebody, but for me it's almost like a prayer. Like just a reminder to myself and those around me that God is good. I love that it's something I'm known for. I walk outside my door wherever I am and Fan Luv tells me bless up and it's a vibe. It just puts a smile on my face when people say it to me. And I like to think it puts a smile on their face when they say it. I've got everyone saying it to me. It's not about what God you worship or what religion you are; it's just about taking a moment to speak on your blessings. It's about all coming together and being thankful for life. The fact that my favorite greeting spreads positivity and gratitude is beautiful. And that I learned this from a place as amazing as Jamaica brings me joy.

I KNEW KHALED from Mixx 96 as one of the most excited and passionate DJs to bless the underground airwaves. At the time he started putting his albums out, we linked up because they needed visuals and they wanted them to look a certain way. I'm from Miami so it just made sense. I did a few smaller videos with him but when we did "We Takin' Over," that really put him on the map. It put us both on the map.

I was working at a big production company in LA and we did a lot of large-scale commercials and some big-budget videos, but this was Khaled's first video and he was on Koch Records, so they didn't have a significant budget. The production company was like, "We can't do what you're envisioning for this. This concept is just too expensive." And I was like, "You don't understand. This is Khaled and he's got every huge artist. This is the biggest thing ever," but they just didn't get it.

So me and Khaled just went down to Miami and reached out to locals. We were just like, "Let's make this happen." We got people to shut down highways for all those driving scenes, we had boat shots, we shot for two days and got that church, and for me personally that video changed everything. I left the company, started my own with my producing partner, Judd Allison, because I could see what we could do ourselves. When people saw the visuals people were just like, "How did he pull that off?" because no one on Koch was making visuals like that. It looked like an $800,000 video, and it was the birth of me and Khaled's relationship. It was madness, but somehow it all came together. We both dream big, and even if no one says we're going to pull it off, we do what it takes. We share this kindred spirit and together we've made so many iconic videos since then, but it's been quite a ride.

And even now I'm not his director on every video—I have my schedule and he has his—but we have this great relationship. He'll call me and send me a video that he just shot and ask me my opinion of it, and we've been through so much and I always want to see him win so we're happy to have the blessings we do.

I'm so proud to be from Miami, and I knew a lot of the artists when they were just coming up like Khaled, Rick Ross, Flo Rida, and Pitbull, so any time there's a Miami music video, there's a certain passion and pride that goes into it for me. In fact the only cameo I've ever made in any video is Khaled's and it's for a song called "Born-N-Raised." It's all about Miami and he insisted that I be in it. I'm not the type of guy that likes my face out there and I prefer to be behind the camera, but that particular video represented Miami and what we all stand for, so I was proud to be in it. Khaled just believes anything can happen and has the work ethic to make it happen, and he's found success with that formula. I'm just so happy for him.

—*Gil Green, director, 305 Films*

BELIEVE IN THE HUSTLE

When I say "Let's win more," I mean we. Just like "We The Best." Not only is it important to big up yourself, you've got to big up everyone else. I'm all about the most ambitious collaborations in my work. But even if you just started following me because of Snapchat and are unfamiliar with my music, you'll know how important Fan Luv is to me. That's also a collaboration.

I love hip-hop. I love the culture. I was a fan first, then a DJ, then I was on radio. I threw parties, and then I became a producer, then an executive, and then an artist. I worked hard, but friendships and teamwork are a huge part of it. I want to win, but I also want everyone who's supported me to win. Major key: Believe in the hustle.

Let me tell you a story about the exact moment my life changed. I had the number one radio show and was DJing in clubs seven days a week, and things started getting a lot better for me. I loved Miami and was so grateful for the opportunities, and it was like everything I'd worked so hard for was all finally coming together. I'd just dropped "We Takin' Over." It was 2007, so this is already almost ten years ago. We were shooting the video, and me and Rick Ross were driving backward in a convertible, reenacting the Puff and Biggie scene from the "Hypnotize" video. As we were driving, I remember turning to Ross with so much joy in my heart and saying, "We made it, man. We made it." Ross turned back to me and said, "This is a movement." We both knew. Ross had dropped "Hustlin'" and we could both feel the energy—we were in.

But, boy, that moment didn't come easy. As my radio career grew I was becoming renowned for breaking records from all over the country in Miami. At that point it was understood that if you had a record break in this city, DJ Khaled had a hand in it. That was how influential my show had become. It's not only that I have the ear for hits, it's that I can see the vision early. I play what I know the people want, but if I love something passionately that's when I go all out. I'll never forget when E-Class, the CEO of Poe Boy Entertainment, came through and brought me "Hustlin'." I was on the radio and the minute I played it I loved it so much I played it for two hours straight. I knew the record was important. I played it and played it again, and after those two hours they suspended me from the radio because I was breaking all the rules and violating protocol. But you couldn't tell me nothing. I just kept saying to my program director that this wasn't about one artist. This was big for the city. I love Miami and the culture here. It's a family; from Trick Daddy to Trina, Flo Rida to Pitbull, the list goes on, and we support each other and we show love. Especially since Trick Daddy's story came before all of us and we have to continue that tradition and pay homage to Dade County.

I believed passionately that it was crucial for me to endorse Miami to everyone who would listen. They told me I'd get suspended for playing it again, so guess what? I played it again. And when I got off suspension I played it again—for two hours—and got suspended again. Every time I got off suspension I just waved that flag for Miami and played the record. This kept going and going and they were ready to fire me but I knew that I had to stand up for what I believed in. This was a storm that needed to be endured.

So when my single "We Takin' Over" came out and we were shooting that video, having Ross beside me, my brother who had climbed this mountain with me, was so meaningful. We've been in this together supporting each other and bigging up this city—me, Ross, E-Class, and Gucci Pucci—for so long, and it's better to have these people share the wins than go it alone. In fact, E-Class, who's a boss, is my business partner in my restaurant Finga Licking. We've all been in the trenches together, from the mud to marble floors.

That record was a movement. And it's so special to me because everybody came through. Akon, T.I., Ross, Fat Joe, Birdman, Lil Wayne . . . everybody was in that video. It didn't matter where you were from; if you were at the height of the game you were on this record. And the vibe was incredible. Nobody was trying to outdo anybody; it was all pure love. If your friends got love for you, your friends will be happy for you when you succeed. That's the difference between we and "they." It's everyone sharing the win. Because wins are happier when you share them. Not only that, wins are bigger when you share them—not smaller. People get this wrong all the time.

For that record there are just so many legendary people. It's what made that record an anthem. Think about it: I had Akon when he was at peak pop culture. He'd crossed over, and trying to get a clearance for him, that's a whole other story, but it came through. At the end of the day you can't deny good music. All these huge artists fight for me to get these clearances, and I have good relationships with the rest of the moguls, so it works out. But let me tell you, in this industry there's always something when it comes to clearances. If you think it's hard to get people to send verses, it's doubly hard to get them to show up for the video shoot and it's five thousand times harder to get clearances. You can lose the record and your mind talking to the label, the label's lawyers, the artist's lawyers—more attorneys than you can ever imagine—and someone always tries to change the deal at the last possible second. The negotiations are endless even if the artist is a friend and signs off on it. Sometimes not being selfish with the wins means you even have to fight to share the win. Especially if you want to make a statement like how Miami's doing it big. But making the most ambitious collaborations in the history of music is what I do. It's all I do. "We Takin' Over" was significant because it validated on a global scale that big collaborations are key for me. I knew I wanted to be an artist and I wanted to be in hip-hop, but it's not like I was going to start writing rhymes. This was the answer. You might not have the exact talent that other people around you have, but you might have another talent. In my case I have a few talents that work together. I have that ear—I know a hit when I hear one. But not only that; I see the hit like it's a blueprint. I know what components I have to bring together so we can share the win. I know who needs to go where—and how they should sound—in order to make that win enormous. Sharing the win is about chemistry. I used to make beats, but now when I say I'm a producer I mean I make sure all the right people come together. I might hear something or I might take a skeleton of an idea and then visualize where all the pieces need to go. When I say my music is like a movie it's because it's big. It has that cinema vibe to it. Especially the videos, but it's also because it's a huge production.

I don't know if you've ever been on a movie set, but sometimes it's a whole city coming together to make something amazing. There's a lot of parts happening at the same time. And it's a lot of jobs. It's also a lot of stress, but I get to make something powerful with my friends, so it's worth it. It's what I do for the culture and it's what I do for Miami—my home.

"Go Harder"

You can see my competitive spirit manifest itself in so many aspects of my career. From my collaborations to my sneaker collection—you can see testaments to my "Go harder" philosophy. If "they" say I can't get summer Jordan 3s, then I'll make sure to get summer Jordan 3s. And don't even get me started on the Eminem 4s. It doesn't matter if it's one of one or one of three hundred; if I want something I'm going to get it.

This is the same drive and positivity I apply to every single one of my collaborations. I want people to see that I can get the rarest, hugest names and the most important voices in one place. Fan Luv knows I go the extra mile to make sure the anthem features dream collaborations. That's what I mean by "Go harder"—go harder than anybody else. Always. It doesn't matter how big you get—you can't be afraid to keep taking risks and never be afraid that people will say no. Every time I make a new record I write down a list of the special cloths I want a verse from. That's my dream list—a handful of names that I haven't been able to convince but that I know one day I'll get. They might always say no or they might change the subject, but I will keep going. Create a list of your own if you need to really focus—if you want to picture your goal—but remember that the only thing standing in the way of go is ego.

DJ KHALED ALWAYS *had that raw energy, that vibe that would lift any track he was playing to a new height. It's great to see Khaled where he is. I was always impressed at how much he loved and embraced our Jamaican culture.*

—*Stephen Marley, Grammy-winning recording artist*

KEEP TWO ROOMS COOKING AT THE SAME TIME

You already know I do every job. I'm a producer, an artist, a CEO—everything—so I know how the machine works when it comes to new music. I'm a boss, so I don't ever get to just be the artist. Other artists might get to imagine themselves floating in outer space, making music, and that's beautiful, but I know what it takes for the whole team to take the product to the next level. I understand the machine; I am the machine. I know they can't do their magic until they have the music. I have successes because I *overstand* both sides.

When I'm in the studio I keep two rooms cooking at the same time. Sometimes when it's crunch time, I'll be cooking in five rooms. You've got to. Meaning as in, I keep that special energy going in as many rooms as needed, and that's a lot of energy. Plus, we hustle around the clock. Sometimes cookin' in two rooms is about having multiple producers finessing tracks in multiple rooms, but sometimes it's about doing as much as you can while you can. When I'm on the road I might be far away from my studio, We The Best Studios, but I always have gear on the tour bus and I always book studios in every city. I'm touring but I'm also recording. It's about being an artist but also a mogul at the same time. It's about making anthems for stadiums but also having restaurants or being in movies to diversify the enterprise.

Sometimes I'll have an hour of sleep, work all day, go to a meeting, then go to the gym, all while I'm on tour in a new city with all these different people that I got to talk to. But if you know me and my team, you'll see how I have my engineer and my director and my photographer with me the whole time.

I care about my career. And I care about my team's careers, so we have to stay alert. This is a twenty-four-hour job that we are blessed to have. Let's get our rest when we need to get our rest, but if it's only ten at night, let's get it in. There's no such thing as there's nothing to do. Let's create something to do. You have to keep cooking when you're hot, and right now we're hot.

I love making music. The music business sometimes drains me because I just want to get to the music, but when you're in my position you've got to get to the business first. That's just how it works. I talk to lawyers every day and every night as an executive. I have artists and producers, so I have to deal with all their deals besides doing my own stuff, which results in a lot of calls and meetings. Sometimes cooking in two rooms is doing two jobs at the same time—jobs that are both important and interconnected. Do one well and the other one prospers, which of course means that you've got to go hard at both.

My team knows all about the benefits of this advice. My artists, my producers, my directors, my people—they always want to do something on the side-hustle tip, too. That's how you keep business boomin'. You got to work around the clock in as many places as possible. "They" don't want me to win, so I'm going to make sure I have every type of win imaginable. It's why I have a popular restaurant business, Finga Licking, and why I have my own headphones. It's absolutely the reason behind why I do all of the We The Best merchandise myself. I see no benefits in outsourcing it to some random third party that we have to pay for the service.

I'm an artist, but managing my own artists, hosting a radio show, and pursuing TV deals and book deals are all part of the larger picture. When I say I'm a mogul I mean it. Keeping two rooms cookin' at the same time keeps your mind sharp because you're never solving the same problem twice. It also puts you in a position where you're keeping track of what's going on in different worlds. Following this philosophy is the foundation of my career.

Collaborations have a lot of parts but learning how to create the best, most iconic wins comes from my love of hip-hop *and* my love of reggae and dancehall. In the early days when I was still flying to Jamaica all the time I would throw parties and participate in soundclashes there. A soundclash is essentially a huge contest with rivaling crews or sound systems, and my DJing experience always made me a vicious contender. My mic game and energy have always been infectious, but the part of the soundclash where I was just unstoppable was getting the most exclusive dubplates. A dub is a one-of-one recording of a hit song that's re-recorded with a new beat and new lyrics that show the competition how relentless you are at getting what you want. The dubs I have with Sizzla, Buju Banton, Capleton, Bounty Killer, and Beres Hammond are the stuff of legend, but where I'd stand out is that I would mix my love of hip-hop and reggae.

Nobody else would take Buju and throw him on top of a DMX Ruff Ryders track. That was like taking the power of two huge hits that were dominating radio at the time and combining them. Not only that, but if you've seen what I'll go through to get a verse, you know my tracks were always on the next level. A rivaling sound system might also have had a Buju Banton dub on a classic rid-dim. I'd go out, get my own, but mine would feature the Marleys on it. This is the point of the soundclash; people couldn't believe what I'd done. Everybody lost their mind. It was signed, sealed, and delivered—I won. This is the at-titude that I bring to everything. I don't just put my crew all on the same song because that's what's expected of me. I put only the best, most powerful people together on a song with the same kind of massive chemistry. This is what producing and making music means to me.

I'm never only doing one thing the same way. If you do that your ideas start becoming routine, and things begin to feel stale. People do this for different reasons. Sometimes it's because of ego. They might think the way they do it is the only right way, and if it worked before, why fix it? But keeping everything exactly as it ever was has never been a sustainable business model. Change always comes. Dinosaurs die.

But another reason people avoid cooking in two rooms is fear. It can be hard for people to put themselves out there, to try something new. I always knew I wanted to act, and in 2002 I had the opportunity to be in a movie; I was in the iconic Jamaican film *Shottas*. It was amazing, even if it was a small part, and now that I'm being asked to consider bigger roles, I'm excited. But all this presents a different kind of pressure. I know these directors don't know what to expect. They don't work in hip-hop and have never met anyone like me, and they don't know the energy. So I have to tell them, "Look, just give me the opportunity. There's nothing to even talk about; you want me to do a screen test? I'll do a screen test. You need me to read a script? Throw me the script—what's the holdup?" I don't stand there telling them I'm too good to read the script. If you're walking into something new and you're cookin' it up in a whole different kind of room, people are going to ask you to do things. They don't know your reputation, but they will.

Don't let their test stand in your way. Show them your natural talent. And if you have to do it a few times for them to see it, don't be embarrassed; just do it. Ask all the questions you need to and make sure you do it right. Keep your attitude positive. Get your foot in the door and then dominate. It's just like any kind of industry.

Do good business, but do it all. If you have a focused vision that has a lot of moving parts, that's beautiful. Don't invest all your energy in one place. It's like financial investments—spread it around. Secure all types of bags. More rooms equal more success, so be kind to the people around you, like your team, and support them and let them cook, too. There's no limit on success. If they have a win that they need my help with, of course I will be there. Cooking in two rooms means being in the trenches in more than one situation. That's called growth and loyalty and it's a major key.

"**L**ionnnnnn!"

Certain Rasta beliefs are amazing to me, like those of Emperor Haile Selassie. He was believed to be the King of Kings, the lion of the tribe of Judah, and he had all these pet lions. You'd see pictures of him petting these lions with long manes, and he was even believed to be able to talk to them. That's just such a powerful image, and one you'll see as a recurring motif in a lot of my work. I love the energy and always admired those beliefs growing up.

I grew up around a lot of Rastas and when we greet each other we'll be like, "Lion Order," as a sign of respect.

Lions are the kings of the jungle and it's a jungle out there, so you've got to be king. You say it to give yourself courage and to invoke that courage in others, too.

You know my house is one of my dreams, but my garden is also one of my dreams. A garden is seasonal, with flowers that have different needs depending on the time of year. I water them and look after them as much as possible, but at the same time I'm never home. While I'm out there on the road securing the bag, my lion, the stone statue you see on my Snapchat, is the protector of my home. Lion watches over my angels and my girl and my yard and my house. My lion represents me, and

I represent the lion. Lion embodies courage and power. It's a constant reminder of what my job is when it comes to my family, but when my queen comes out and sees Lion, I want her to feel safe and know I'm coming home soon. Plus, he's just somebody for me to talk to when I'm thinking about the pathway to more success. Lion talk is a major key, for real.

SUCCESS DOESN'T HAPPEN by accident, but rather through deliberate daily action. Optimum wellness is the same, and is a very important key to success. The first step toward optimum wellness is . . . well, a step. Khaled has made taking that first step easy, fun, entertaining, and possible through his inspirational ways. He puts aside vanity in an effort to empower the world with a feeling of inclusivity that makes everyone feel like they, too, can do it. Khaled's step toward wellness is one that has caused a ripple around the world that will turn into a seismic shift toward conscious living, not only through conversation, but also action.

—Marco Borges, bestselling author, trainer, and founder of 22 Days Nutrition

TEMPTATION IS A TYPE OF "THEY"

I take the responsibility of being a role model super seriously. You got to. I know some people don't welcome what they feel to be added pressure, but I think it's a blessing to be visible in this way. It's not about creating any expectations to be perfect. It's that being a role model helps me stay focused so that I'm deserving of Fan Luv's love.

Temptation is definitely a "they." I told you "they" takes all forms in various situations, and temptation is one of the hardest things to resist. It can be anything—food, other women, drugs, or alcohol. I don't want Fan Luv or people I respect or do business with catching me out there looking wild. The way I see it, I'm a boss—a don—and you can't maintain that level of respect if you're going out and looking out of control. You'll notice that I never get drunk or wild out—that ain't me.

On the occasions that I see people I know out there doing all the crazy stuff, I'm disappointed. I don't know why someone would play themselves in front of a live audience and a sea of iPhones. Those images and that footage can live forever. Mess around at the wrong time, and the visual of you playing yourself could become a meme. People don't have privacy anymore, even without going out in public and acting up in front of all them cameras. I've been in the game for over twenty years, but I don't have drama or rumors about my personal life out there. Why? Because when it comes to drugs and getting drunk or women, I don't mess with it. I've always been the type of person who's on point. You never know who's out there so I don't advertise any signs of weakness. But it's not just about who's watching; discipline has to happen all the time, or at least most of the time, and that's just for yourself. I'm not trying to tell anyone what they can and can't do, or that everything is bad. God gave man the ability to choose—free will is a beautiful thing. I drink to celebrate, but I don't get drunk. That's the difference. I always tell you to celebrate responsibly, and that's what I mean. I'm going to be honest with you: Once you get to be a boss, you really start thinking about your time in a different way. I make sure I spend time at home with my family and resting so that I can make the best decisions. Even when I'm out celebrating, I might do it to glorify the successes of the people around me. It's good for your team to have fun and feel the moment and get hyped about the next win.

But for me, even while I celebrate I'm thinking about the next win. When I'm in my sanctuary on my hammock or in my Jacuzzi, I'm genuinely relaxed, but if I'm in a nightclub or out at a party, I'm watching everything.

It's not that I don't enjoy life, but I don't have time for regrets. Plus, I've seen drugs kill ambition, ruin reputations, and even destroy God-given genius. Let me tell you, when I think about the temptations that have ruined talent, it breaks my heart.

Maybe it's because I've been in the game for so long or because my work has always been my passion, but I've always kept my eye on the bag. My whole life is dedicated to making sure that people are listening to incredible music and having fun. When I throw parties or DJ, I make sure to tear it up. But I'm older now, and even though I never thought I'd be the type of person to tell the young world to be careful, I know I need to tell all of you not to fall in the trap. Once you fall in the trap, you have to invest so much time and energy getting out. And that's if you even get out. If you get caught up too early, that's not securing the bag.

Of course I know that when you're young you think you're going to live forever and that your mistakes can get fixed. Be free to make mistakes. Go big. Learn. But don't make that one mistake that stops you from seeing the opportunity that changes your life. Getting caught up in drugs and alcohol is a type of mistake that makes it too easy to make the next hundred mistakes. Don't play yourself at the worst possible time. Don't lose the most important years of school or work that might lead you to the biggest wins of your life. Timing is everything. I'm grateful because my family raised me right. I never did drugs. I never tried Molly, pills, none of that. I truly believe it's always easier to say no from the beginning than to try to say it later. I always had different interests. Winning, to me, is the ultimate good time. That might sound corny, but it's true.

I know that resisting is a challenge, and it's okay to be curious about what it's like, but I just think of the bigger picture. The bigger picture is paradise—my backyard, my musical garden, being home by the ocean; that's paradise to me. Now that I have it, I'm not going to let anything bad happen to it. You got to protect the good in your life.

When you're young you might be distracted by all the fun you think you're missing out on, but keep your mind on where you want to be next. Put your head down and work. Besides, drugs are serious. It's not just about people watching and judging you; drugs are the devil. I don't want the devil in me.

God gave you life, and life is a blessing. When I read about all the young people who lose their lives and are taken too early, it makes me think. I think about all the great accomplishments they could have experienced. I think about all the amazing music, art, or technology they could have made, or the books they could have written. All this knowledge that makes the world richer is gone. They could have been the next Obama, the next Oprah, the next person who is so special that we don't even know their name yet! You've got to watch your back out there, and it's always easier to do it when you're not all messed up.

"Stay Fresh"

If you want to be treated like a boss, you've got to look the part. Get a fresh cut twice a week. In fact, when I'm having a significant week sometimes I get three haircuts. Taking a half hour just for myself to think about life lends me a sharper perspective on the upcoming deals. Look, I know how it is when you're trying to put food on the table, and in those moments a haircut can feel like a luxury or an unnecessary expense, but my point is: Make time. Even if it's just going to see your boy who knows how to cut hair, go get a shape-up. Make grooming part of your ritual. It's like putting your game face on; it builds confidence and gets your mind in the right zone. On that note, cocoa butter is also a major key when it comes to self-care. People always ask me why I smell so good, and the answer is Palmer's cocoa butter. I don't wear cologne.

Being mindful about presentation doesn't mean that everyone is shallow or has vanity problems, or that you need to change everything about your appearance to fit in. You've got to put in work and be smart and humble, but humans make snap judgments, so don't get in your own way. Don't get dismissed based on something as amateur as looking sloppy. Cloth talk can happen when you least expect it, and if your appearance looks put together, you'll feel more confident in your ideas. Your thoughts will be more focused and you won't be distracted.

So get a fresh cut twice a week and definitely before an executive decision. And when you're ready and you graduate to the next level, get a pedicure and a manicure once a week, too.

*I **IMMEDIATELY CONNECTED** with Khaled's energy and charisma—he's funny, open, and real. We laughed together and began planning to build his empire, but of course twenty minutes later, five hundred of his fans showed up. If that doesn't confirm the power of his connection with his audience, I don't know what does.*

—Jeremy Zimmer, CEO, United Talent Agency

FAN LUV

I call my fans Fan Luv because that's the feeling I get when they're around—love. For real. Fan Luv is a definite blessing, and loving Fan Luv is a major key. For me, it's an easy key, because that's just my personality. I love meeting new people. When Fan Luv happens, I'm just grateful. It doesn't matter if I'm in a meeting or I'm in a restaurant eating; if you try to meet me, I will try to meet you. Everybody needs inspiration, and my inspiration is life, but it's really my fans and my family who inspire me to go hard. Every time I see Fan Luv it's a reminder to go in. And I want them to do the same. Fan Luv is everything to me, for real. That's always been the case, but these past few years I've come to understand how powerful Fan Luv can really be.

The thing about me is that I'm usually on the road every year from February until November. That's the life of a DJ and an artist and it's been my working life for about as long as I can remember. When we're just on the road—hustling, touring, being in the studio, making albums, dropping records—the months take on a certain rhythm and the cities and states blur by. Every year we do it again, just bigger, but I make it a point to be home for the holidays. My birthday's during Thanksgiving time (shout-out to Sagittariuses!) and usually the buildings, meaning the executives and the music labels, shut down from around Thanksgiving to Christmas. So I come home and chill.

This is when I just do me—working in the studio, spending as much time as possible in my musical garden, lounging in the hammock, and for the first time last year I was Snapchatting. Snapchat is a major key and a game-changer, but what I like about it most is that it's not about the angle or editing or lighting or how good you look, it's just you for ten seconds being real with your fans.

So I'm Snapchatting, vibing, and people are hitting me up with feedback like, "Yo, Khaled, I love your Snapchat!" I even get a call from Ed Sheeran. He's like, "Lion!" Just saying *lion* into my phone, and I'm like, "Oh, Ed, word. You know about that lion." And he's telling me he loves my energy, and I'm like, "Thank you, I appreciate it."

One day I'm out there Jet Skiing because I love the ocean. Since Rick Ross lives nearby on the water I go over there on my Jet Ski for lunch. We're having a good time, but when I start heading back to my house I realize it's getting dark. Before long it's pitch-black and I get lost. I'm just out there by myself, using the light on my phone to see. Meanwhile, I'm keeping my sense of humor and Snapchatting because I've got to stay focused and because I won't lie to you, I was getting a little scared.

Major key for real: Don't drive your Jet Ski in the dark.

Finally I make it home, God bless, and my phone's acting crazy. Of course it broke because of all that salt water getting into it. So the next day I go to the Apple Store in my swim trunks and my flip-flops and since I'm DJ Khaled, I get love. People ask for pictures and autographs, and I'm blessed to have that in my career, but while I'm at the Apple Store getting my phone fixed I turn around to take a snap and realize that the whole mall is crammed inside the store with me. This was my first time coming out of the house because I was on some hibernation vibes, so I thought this was strange. I'm wondering what's going on and looking around thinking Justin Bieber is in the store or something. But then a few kids start talking to me and then a few more and I figure out that it's Fan Luv, but just with a new kind of energy. There were just so many of them, and they had all been watching my Snapchat. Come to find out some of them even hit up the coast guard to call a search party for me. All these people were saying my name and calling themselves "Fan Luv" and they're talking about my flowers and my Jet Skis and I'm just blown away.

Still, that was home, and I'm used to a certain amount of attention in Miami, so it wasn't until I went to Vegas to DJ at Tao for New Year's Eve that I knew things had really changed. I don't fly, so I get there on my tour bus and I get up to the hotel and I walk into the lobby and a few people are like, "Yo, Khaled! Yo, Khaled! Yo, Khaled!" and I'm like, "Love. Love. Love," just giving pounds and walking through because I'm exhausted. I go to my room to sleep and don't really think anything of it.

When I wake up, I'm like, "Let's go test this vibe; I'm in Vegas." So I come downstairs and there's a huge crowd of people by the elevator; I just walk through and the owner of the club is like, "Yo, you can't come out here." And I don't get it. It was my second year doing this event so I just look at him like he's confused and keep it moving. That's when—boom—I see it. It's just a wall of Fan Luv.

Just a whole sea of people wanting to meet me and I'm just humbled by the intensity of their love.

I tell people all the time that Snapchat changed my life. I've been on the covers of business magazines and on talk shows about it. Tech people ask me how it is that I became such a huge force on the app but what I need everyone to *overstand* is that social media is nothing without people. It's not that Snapchat changed my life, Fan Luv changed my life. That's why no matter what I'm doing, where I go, or how big I get, I will never take Fan Luv for granted. My team gets on me all the time because I take so long getting from place to place because I'm shaking as many hands as possible and taking as many selfies as possible, but I can't stop. Some of my closest friends think I'm crazy for letting Fan Luv into my life but I just remember that Fan Luv helps me. When I was lost—literally lost—they gave me strength and guidance. How can I ever forget or be ungrateful about everything they've done for me? So I love Fan Luv and will always love Fan Luv. There's no other way. So don't ride your Jet Ski in the dark, but if you do, make sure you have your phone because that flashlight is a key. But the real *major* key? Make sure you've got good people looking out for you.

"Have a Lot of Pillows"

"They" don't want you to have a lot of pillows, so I make sure to have a lot of pillows. It is a major key to rest your greatness.

Pillows are important. When you sleep, you're supposed to sleep like a king or a queen, and every time you turn there should be something comfortable to greet you. And that softness reminds all the parts of your body that it's time to relax. You've seen me work. You know I'm always either in the studio or on tour. I'm always cooking something or pushing myself at the gym, so no matter if I've got one hour or two hours or four hours, I make sure I sleep right.

A lot of us don't have a lot of pillows. I didn't have a lot of pillows growing up. Let me tell you, I had no pillows when I slept in that Honda. Plus, when I got an apartment all I had was my music, and I had no pillows. I would have my one sheet and I'd rest my head on records. I don't recommend it. So you know one of the first things I did when the wire hit was get a couple pillows. Everyone has a different idea of luxury when they first get a little money. One person might only wear brand-new sweat socks every single day. Another might eat Cheesecake Factory for every meal for like a month. Me, I got a lot of pillows. They remind me of when I didn't have pillows, so I'm grateful for all of them.

When you're a self-made mogul, the temptation to work all the time no matter how tired you feel is high. Ten years ago you couldn't tell me nothing. I wouldn't sleep for days. Now, I'm not going to lie to you, when the pressure is on and I'm recording an album or planning the next major deal, I might work thirty hours straight, but I don't make a habit of it. Pillows are like the angels of my bedroom.

FOR FAR TOO long, I subscribed to a very flawed definition, buying into our collective delusion that burning out is the necessary price for accomplishment and success. Too many years of this led to my painful wake-up call: Sleep-deprived and exhausted, I fainted, hit my head on my desk, and broke my cheekbone. I was on the cover of magazines and had been chosen by *Time* as one of the world's one hundred most influential people. But after my fall I had to ask myself, was this what success looked like? Was this the life I wanted?

We all want to perform at the top of our game, every day—to "be great and keep being great," as Khaled puts it. For me, a more sustainable and fulfilling kind of success was understanding that not only is there no trade-off between living a well-rounded life and high performance, performance is actually improved when our lives include time for rest and renewal. It's a major key.

> —*Arianna Huffington, bestselling author*
> *and founder of the* Huffington Post

INSPIRE THE YOUNG WORLD

There's never been a time when a young king or a young queen approached me in the street that it didn't make me smile. Now, I have love for all of Fan Luv, no matter your age, but if I get to have an impact on young people's lives, I know that's a real blessing. I've been doing this for a long time but when I say I'm just getting started, I mean it. I'm excited to see where I'll be in five years, or even ten, just knowing where I've been. But the part that makes me really grateful is that new fans, fans who are too young to know about my past wins, still find me and have love for me.

But it's not all about fans; it's about the new generation. When you've been in the game as long as I have and you get older, you really start thinking about the people coming next. Some people, once they get a few wins, get selfish. They start only thinking about themselves and how they're going to hold on to everything they worked hard for, and a lot of the time they do this by keeping everybody out. They start looking over their shoulder and seeing the young as "they." For the most part it's a sure sign of insecurity, and the result is that they start getting competitive instead of being a teacher.

That's just a cycle. And it's a negative one. That's how you produce generations that haven't learned anything about the business and the culture. That's how you have whole groups of people who don't know how to respect the code, because they were never treated with respect. They had to fight and break down doors for everything, too, and then you have an entire industry that's frustrated and bitter. That's how beefs start, and unfortunately that's how a culture erodes and becomes weaker. That's the part of the story that makes my heart heavy. Think about it: We all came together because we have love for the same music and the same interests, but eventually egos and emotions get in the way. My albums are the few moments in a crazy, competitive landscape where everyone gets along for the sake of the anthem.

I'm speaking on music when I say this, but this goes for all cultures and all industries. It's the same way in TV or magazines or movies. You've got old people mad at the new people coming up on the Internet. It's always been a cycle, for hundreds of years, no matter what game you were in. Even with factories, people built cars and then the machines took over. Old and new always fight when innovation changes the ways things are. It's just that these days, the innovations come faster and faster. This can be scary to some people, but to me this just means the opportunities come faster and faster. I love the new era. It's all about perspective and it's all about looking forward, not back.

What the older generation sometimes forgets because they're too busy maintaining their status is that new people can teach you things. It's called not being a dinosaur. It's why all the moguls I work with stay relevant and know what's next. Someone might have had to help me figure out Snapchat, but look what that did for me. Sometimes the next success really comes from a place where you least expect it. Some people might think Snapchat is silly or a waste of time, but just from one app, I have more people following me than some TV shows have audience members. Tell me you're going to say no to that or deny it. Especially when all you're doing is broadcasting something you're already doing, like talking to your lion, loving Fan Luv, or Jet Skiing. That's like getting paid twice.

But once you get to where I am, with the amount of experience I have, you start thinking of the next generation in a different way. I love working with new artists. It's my job, because I want to find new talent and work with them on my label. Hits are timeless. But once you start working with someone who comes from a different generation, you can start thinking about music in new ways. When I was coming up, where you came from really mattered, and it really made an impact on your sound. That's not happening anymore. Producers can make any market sound like them no matter what artists they're working with. Plus, new artists can put music into the world so easily. The Internet can really level the playing field.

Technology changed the game just because there are so many new ways to discover and request music. I come from radio and still have a radio show, so all this is interesting to me. I need to stay on top of all this and master it.

I love hip-hop. It gave me so much, and in so many ways it raised me. It brought me so many opportunities, and it brought me so many friends. Friends who are my family. I want the culture to stay that way. In my lifetime I've seen rap go from being an almost underground culture to cross over and become pop. Everyone listens to hip-hop now; that's just the way it is. But I want to make sure that the culture—the heart and the soul of the industry—survives.

That's why I think it's so critical to have a relationship with not only the people who came before you and the people who you came up with, but also the people who are next. You want the culture to grow; this is how to influence the way it grows. You want the culture to become prosperous and wise, and you want it to evolve, and you want as many people as possible to move with a clean heart and do good business. You want the leaders to lead by example and the new guard to teach those who come after them.

I want love to influence people—not fear and greed. And the only way I can do that is to be a role model for the people who work with me and the people who see me on social media every day.

Now, I'm nowhere near perfect, and I know that. I never finished high school. I even tried to go back and get my GED, but that didn't work out. I just couldn't get back in that mind-set after I started on my career. And a lot of the things I learned, I had to learn outside of a classroom, and no matter the storms I weathered, I met a lot of good people who influenced me, and that's a blessing. I just want to make sure I pass along that same blessing to young kings and young queens so they can teach the next generation. Also, I hope anyone reading this stays in school, because let me tell you: It's real hard to go back.

"It's a Cold World, Bundle Up"

You know when you got out of the shower and your mother always said, "Dry your back"? That's because it's a cold world. Dry your back so you don't get sick, but also watch your back. Bundle up even when it's summertime because the world is cold. Go that extra mile to make sure to protect yourself. Sometimes I imagine the young world out there and think about how Fan Luv will somehow get this message from me. Maybe you're just driving your car to work or school and I'm on the radio. Maybe you hear my voice saying "It's a cold world, dry your back" on Instagram or Snapchat. That might not even make any sense to you. You might repeat it a few times to yourself because my keys are catchy. You might not even be thinking about it as it applies to real life. But trust me, that's gonna cook in your head. You'll laugh or giggle thinking about how I'm telling you to bundle up even when the sun's shining, but later on you're going to say, "Man . . . this shit is real!" because that world is going to get you. "They" is real. Trouble is real. My keys aren't just memes or catchphrases; they're real life. The cold world can be colder than you can ever imagine until you have to live through it. Be aware. Be extra aware. Don't say it like it's a game, do it—dry your back *and* watch your back. Don't be cocky, and stay prepared. When you see this come to light you're going to know that what Khaled said is real. It's just too real.

CHOOSE YOUR OWN WINS

You're special cloth and you're breaking down doors by being yourself, so the next major key is to choose your own wins. What does that even mean? It means you've got to risk it all and bet on yourself. That doesn't mean you can't collaborate with people on big ideas. It means that when push comes to shove, you have to look out for yourself first, and part of that is knowing your worth.

Before the We The Best Epic deal—which is the deal I have now—I was a free agent. This was new to me. From the day I dropped my first album I was fortunate enough that legendary people like Fat Joe looked out for me and cosigned me so I could be on Koch Records. But then when I started my own label, We The Best Music Group, sometimes I would be on a label as an artist myself, "DJ Khaled," but We The Best and my artists would be a part of another company. This new deal with Epic that I signed to create We The Best/Epic is the first time I have everything in one place.

So why wouldn't everyone want to be a free agent all the time? Because freedom has a price. It's just like any other game out there; the more freedom you have, the more risks you have to take. It's choosing the harder road and being confident enough in yourself that you'll see that risk pay off. That means that I, as an artist, was a free agent, but also my label was a free agent, which meant that I personally had to be the security net for everybody.

But here's the thing: I'd worked my whole life for this moment and I was ready. Even as the stress built up on my shoulders and everybody was looking at me nervously, I knew I could do this. Because guess what? There was no alternative. I had to ask myself every day, "Who gonna help feed me and my family if I don't have the means?"

When you're a boss, you have to help people out, but no one's gonna carry you but God. That's no disrespect to anyone, but the question you have to ask before breaking off and betting on yourself is: Do you have the strength to stand alone? Not only that but do you have the strength to carry your team and your family when you stand alone? If the answer is no, you might not be ready.

For years I broke barriers. I put out smash-hit records at every step of my career and at each new level I made sure to learn a different job. By the time I went out on my own I knew about being a producer, an A&R man, a record executive, radio, working at a record store, even how a record would sound when I dropped it on a dance floor—everything—because in the past I had to do it all. Being independent meant I spent a lot of energy doing everything, but it also meant I got better at a variety of skills. It's funny, but let me tell you, when you're putting your own money up and betting on yourself, you *over-stand* every job that needs to get done real quick. You're learning on your own dime and in that situation it pays to learn fast.

If I partnered with somebody in the past, I definitely salute them, but I always took the big risks on my own. I have to be honest about that. I'm not saying various people didn't rep for me but I put my money where my mouth is. I gambled on my life and made every investment out of pocket. Meaning if I made money, the minute that money came I would put it right back into the company. For many years I sacrificed personal things to keep the lights on at work. Doubling down on your business is choosing your own win, and when you're independent, you've got to live lean. It's called securing the bag.

But let me tell you why God is the greatest. When I decided to go out and bet on myself it had been ten years of We The Best Music Group. There were deals on the table and they were fine, but they weren't the deals I deserved so I walked away. That was me making a statement not only to the industry but to myself; I wanted to see what I was capable of on my own. Well, during this one year where my label and I were free agents out of the twenty-plus years I've been in this game, my career skyrocketed. Everything exploded at exactly the right time. Snapchat happened, Jay Z became my manager, I got to go on tour with Beyoncé, I had huge new deals come in one by one, and since I was experiencing all of this success while I was out on my own, I could dictate my own worth. I pray and give thanks constantly when I think about the odds.

Plus, even the fact that I have this deal with L.A. Reid is meaningful to me. This is the man who gave me my first executive job when he positioned me as president of

Def Jam South, but he also gave me my first label deal. It always humbled me so much that a music mogul like L.A. saw the vision early and was confident in my abilities as a boss. And the fact that when he left Def Jam one of his first orders of business as CEO of Epic was to call me makes me feel so incredibly blessed. Let me tell you, God really moves in mysterious ways. There were so many stars that had to align to result in this historical event that created We The Best/Epic and I'm so grateful they did.

So when I talk about how you should bet on yourself, I really know what I'm talking about. Anyone who tries to scare you into staying where you are or taking a bad deal really is a "they."

I'm in a win-win position right now that's making all the storms and the hardship worth it. When you can part-ner with someone who's already a boss, it's incredible. I trust L.A.'s vision, and he knows mine and supports it. He can take some of the hits, and this is a man who also knows how to make hits. I'm phenomenal now, but in order for me to get here I had to take risks. I had to choose my own win, meaning I had to risk it all and ride for me. "They" tried to take my vision apart and tell me that my business wasn't as valuable as I knew it to be. "They" were trying to bargain with me about my future, and now "they" really know that I'm not to be played with when it comes to my dreams.

The labels understood me as the artist. I had to make them *overstand* me as the boss. I couldn't fold. That's a major key. If you spend all these years ripping down doors and betting on yourself, why would you take a bad deal after all that work?

But man, this path hasn't been easy and sometimes it's hard to see the light. These dark days will test you, so you just have to have faith that you made the right decision for your vision. When you're a boss, sometimes you got to put yourself in the storm to get out of it. And these storms get big. At times like these everybody around me might think I'm crazy, but look at where I'm at now. The sun is shining and life is beautiful. When you choose your own wins, you're right where you're supposed to be.

"Don't Burn No Bridge; Only God Can Walk on Water"

Can you walk on water? I didn't think so. Only God can walk on water, so don't burn no bridge. This sounds obvious as a piece of advice because no man is an island, but it's also very easy advice to forget in the moment. Burning a bridge might be lying at your job or being disloyal. Those are some of the quickest ways to burn a bridge with me from a business standpoint, but the other way to burn bridges is not making the bridge in the first place—to fail at making those vital connections. I'm in a situation right now where I meet a lot of people. There's just a lot of rooms, sets, and buildings with a lot of new faces and new opportunities that might require a new skill. I might have to read a teleprompter for my lines or hit my mark or really get my acting on. In these moments I might not know exactly what the director wants, so I just ask. I'll ask everyone on set. I'll ask the other actors I'm working with, like Ray Liotta or Naomi Campbell, and make sure to take the time to ensure that our collaboration makes everybody excited. What I mean is: Not only don't burn no bridge; always make bridges. Open yourself up. Establish connections when you can—that's the beauty of collaborations. Some people are closed off, and while I understand that it might be their personality, a lot of the time it's because they're scared or insecure. It's like they want to act like their bridges have a million-dollar toll because they'd rather seem like they have all the answers and all the resources they need on their own. People need people. Period. Not only that, people need people especially when they're making big moves. Only God can walk on water, but also God is the only one who doesn't need anyone else. The day you can make the whole entire world and all living things and consciousness and bridges like God can, maybe then you can think about setting fire to one.

I GIVE WHAT I like to receive without compromising who I am. People love and respect that I give love without looking like I want something in return. I've been blessed tremendously in my life, I don't need anything from anybody other than that. I have children and a family. But family isn't just necessarily about your blood relatives. It's the people who have been positioned in your life to have the consistency of mutual love, mutual respect, and that genuine mutual concern.

Khaled does exactly what I speak about and I can only interact with those kinds of people. There's a principle. There's just a right way to live by—laws that govern man—there's a right and wrong. No matter what language you speak, everybody knows that when you strike someone it's not the right way unless that person threatened your well-being on a physical level. There's just certain things that everybody knows are right regardless of your color, your culture, and your upbringing.

I like to be peaceful. I love love, I really do. That's been the driving force and the fire that burns inside of me because everything ain't always about the business. Now we have the opportunity to be in the music industry and turn our love and passion into a business, but before, you weren't getting no money, it was just love. If people loved your rhymes and they loved your songs and your performance, they would acknowledge their love for what you did, and that shit went a long way. It was a priceless reward.

I love seeing people happy and I'm grateful. Khaled is the same way. That person on camera is exactly who he is, and he finally got a chance to show people. As entertaining as it may be, the love that he receives is because Khaled isn't waking up every day trying to provide a script to a film about some character. He doesn't have to practice this shit. He doesn't have to try to remember a script. He doesn't have to be reminded of what his lines are each day. This is exactly who he has been for the twenty years that I've known him, which is why long before Snapchat he was able to rally people together to create the most incredible collabs for his albums. Then and now. People always wondered how he was able to get everybody, but this Khaled guy is such a giver of love and such a giver of incredible, feel-good energy. He gets the best out of people. People love and trust him. Now, I'm not going to say I haven't seen him put his foot down and scream on a muthaf*cka, because he has a business to run. Sometimes you've got to rule with an iron fist, but his love and his happiness come back tenfold.

I genuinely trust Khaled with my life. He's just one

of those people that I hold in high regard because he acts on all the right ways to deal with people. You really don't have a choice but to rise above the day-to-day bullshit because nothing is supposed to be perfect. If you didn't have challenges you wouldn't even have a journey or a story to tell. You won't learn the value of the struggle or the rewards of the success when they come. I was definitely taught that failure is not an option and I attribute that to my mother and father. We all go through bullshit but at the end of the day we also know that it could be a lot worse so don't run around and complain. Don't bitch. Resolve it because you have no choice. Especially if people are relying on you because you're the source of everyone's well-being.

It's not just necessarily about being the boss. It's about being the provider. I can't tell my mother what to do; she's still the boss and that boss shit don't work in my mother's house, but it's about what you represent—as a man, as a human being, and as an individual who stands for what you stand for. Be worthy of that respect from others. I try to represent that leadership and it has to do with my family, but it has a lot to do with the greats who came before me that I aspire to: Chuck D, Elijah Muhammad, Malcolm X, Marcus Garvey, Martin Luther King. I could go on. In order to be a leader you have to command the respect that will allow people to anoint you to lead them. I don't like to be around anything that condones or causes bullshit. I do not like liabilities. You can't walk around and claim yourself as a leader if you don't do the shit that earns respect.

—*Busta Rhymes, rapper and hip-hop pioneer*

KEEP IT OFF THE RECORD

Start every conversation you have, including ones with your best friend, by saying, "This is off the record." It might sound paranoid or like you're doing too much, but truly, you never know who's listening, and you never know who's watching. You don't need me to tell you that there are cameras and recording devices everywhere these days. It doesn't matter if you're a celebrity or not; don't play yourself.

It might be surprising that I would talk about the benefits of keeping it off the record since I'm on Snapchat or social media in general all the time. But there's a time and a place for everything. That's where I give my fans Khaled unfiltered. Matter fact, that's what I love about Snapchat—that it's just me, no rehearsals. And I love inviting Fan Luv into my home and certain aspects of my life. But when it comes to my family, I keep it all off the record. You've got to. Why would I air out my family's personal information and everything about my mama's business? She didn't choose this lifestyle for herself, and I don't invite people to bother my parents, my siblings, or my girl. All the great ones know when to keep it off the record. President Obama knows; he wouldn't let me Snapchat in the White House even though I had a perfect angle all set up for cloth talk.

Bosses know that when you're working on something you've got to keep that information classified. Until the wire hits, you can't let anyone know what you've got cooking. It doesn't matter if it's music or any other industry; you can't let anything leak before you get the clearance. People might want to try to steal the bag. Or a "they" might come along and ruin it just because "they" want to end you. I make sure to look around me if I'm playing something sensitive in the studio. Or if I'm about to get on the phone with my lawyer and talk about a deal in front of someone I don't know, I might never even say the name of who we're talking about if it's an artist. Or I might just call the new deal "the deal," so like, "What's the status on the deal we was talking about?" It's my lawyer or my manager; they know what I'm talking about, which bag I'm waiting on.

Plus, if we're in the studio I make sure everybody isn't tweeting or gramming or recording anything that they can then go ahead and leak, whether it's on purpose or by accident. Sometimes a leak can work for you and sur-prise you. When my song "I'm So Hood" leaked, it wasn't even cleared yet, and I was so stressed out thinking I might get sued, but it became such an undeniable smash on the streets. When that leaked it was a surprise. But I don't like thinking that someone around me didn't keep things tight until I said it was a go. Meaning, these are not the kind of surprises I like. Matter fact, I rarely like surprises period. The other part of keeping it off the re-cord is to never disrespect anybody on social media. This is something everyone can control. We're all old enough to know better and it's just good business. Your conduct on social media lets a lot of potential business associates know what you're about. With that in mind, sometimes I can't even believe the types of code violations going on in the mentions. For real, I can't contain my disappointment with people sometimes. Major key: If you have a situation, you pick up the phone. You set up a meeting and you talk among grown men or grown women. You do it boss style. If you have a problem, bring it to the table, meaning no violence. Going back and forth on social media is a waste of emotion and energy. Bosses don't take it to the com-ments. We find solutions.

Social media is for positivity, to spread Fan Luv. Not to downgrade people publicly. It confuses me sometimes that grown men and grown women put each other on blast. They're starting beef, talking about all types of personal matters and sensitive business, and people who aren't even a part of the conversation start being dragged in. Random people weigh in with their unsolicited opinions and small issues blow up.

I can't imagine a bigger waste of time. Who has all this energy to stir things up? People who aren't successful and people who aren't working hard, that's who.

Plus, social media isn't the place to start shit. It's designed to heighten misunderstanding. One person says something, someone else responds, and pretty soon the Internet is reporting it. Why would you want your name to be tied to some pettiness instead of your wins and accomplishments? That kind of hostility is like poison, and it spreads fast. Fans start losing respect for you or start going in on other fans. The escalation infuriates everybody, and it makes everybody look crazy. That's why I love Fan Luv. We get along and spread positivity.

But it's not just public beefs between famous people that I'm talking about. I don't understand the news cycle at all these days. Seriously. You'd think there were more important things to talk about than this kind of drama when it comes to regular people turning on each other, too. In fact, I know there are more important things given the inequality of our country. Yet all manner of trash keeps getting blown up. All that disrespect takes shine away from the positive aspects of humanity and all the good we do. I want my message to be love and I want my legacy to be a big heart.

That's what's sad to me. I'm all about peace and unity, and this kind of public negativity breeds more public negativity. That's what I mean by escalation. It's like if all you do is eat junk food, it's all you're going to want to eat. It's like training yourself to make bad decisions. You're just getting caught up in a cycle of evil and wanting to be in someone else's business when you've got business of your own you need to attend to. Plus, junk food doesn't ever make you full. Real talk.

Whenever I see someone tear someone else down on social media it just shows me that they're not happy. If you're not happy, change it. Start a new project or get a hobby. It might feel like all the attention you're getting online is real, but it's not. People who want you to be negative all the time are not really your friends.

Another part of keeping it off the record is that your whole team needs to know that this is how you conduct business. This has to be second nature to them too. We The Best is a family, and some of these people I've known for years. Matter fact, some of them have been my friends since I was fifteen. Starting a business is tough, and if you work with people that long, you're going to fight—especially when it's growing pains. That's just a part of life. We could argue all day about something, but not only do we squash it, you won't hear about it anywhere, ever. This trust is so important. This bond is what will determine your greatness as a team.

Plus, no member of my team will ever take any negativity—even if it's directed to someone else—to the timeline. It's a negative reflection on the rest of us. I truly believe that.

This key is for everyone. It's not just about professional relationships. It doesn't matter if you're forty or fourteen. Keeping your face clean and being reliable and positive even with your friends is what you want to be known for. And if you're lucky like I am, you might grow up to do business with those friends and prosper. Believe me, it's one of the best feelings in the world.

"Ownership Is Key"

If you see me on Snapchat you know I love to Jet Ski. I always Jet Skied if I ever went on vacation as a kid, so I love it. It reminds me of vacations with my family. But now I don't have to wait my turn or rent someone else's, because guess what? I own my Jet Ski. I also own my golf cart.

If you've got a mortgage, you've got to pay interest. People think if you pay a mortgage, most of that money goes to the principal. The principal is the price tag. But unless you buy it straight-up, what you pay every month is mostly interest. That's you being owned by a bank. You really can end up paying forever. If you have opportunities to be an owner, take it.

Ownership is important. It's not about just having things for a couple of months, it's about keeping them. I work in the music industry. The difference between people who get fifteen minutes of fame and the people who thrive and take care of their team for a long time is that bosses own their music. Not everyone is going to be in the position to own, but if you can own part of it, make sure you do. Fight for it—even if people try to tell you you don't deserve it or try to bully you into handing it over. It's not just entertainment; this is everything. Don't think about just the next six months of your life, think about the next sixty years. Owning something is always better even if it's easier to rent or easier to have someone own it and lend it to you. You want the security of ownership, even if you're young and think you have all the time in the world to figure your life out, because you never know what's going to happen.

Workers work. Bosses own.

MY FIRST IMPRESSION *of Khaled was, "This dude gotta be insane." He's just got crazy ideas. It's a different time now and we're getting the right treatment and shit's big, but that speaks to the moves that we were discussing and the moves we were making. Khaled's a hard worker. He's dedicated. He gave his life to the culture and he's been dedicated from day one. He supported me from the very first single I released and even before. There's so many different reasons I would love to continue to collaborate with my brother. And his keys? His keys are free game. He's just giving it out, so a lot of dudes need to put 'em on their key ring.*

—Rick Ross, rapper and founder of Maybach Music Group

GLORIFY YOUR OWN SUCCESS

I told you that everything that's happening right now, I believed it into existence. "They" don't want you to win, so I'm gonna make sure to win.

I told you the benefits of being humble. Be humble when it comes to learning from others, be humble when it comes to respecting the code and the culture, be humble in your life and your relationship with God, but every time there's a new deal alert and every time that wire hits, you've got to glorify your success. Not only is nobody else going to do it for you, you have to show everyone that you stand behind your ventures.

You've seen me. I've got huge announcements every week. Just look at these names: Jay Z, Beyoncé, Epic, Apple, Penguin Random House. Do you think it's easy to secure joint ventures like these? Well, it ain't. Stakes are high, and as I've taught you, "they" are everywhere.

The key is to tell Fan Luv *and* "they" every time you have another win.

It's validating for you and your team to take time to think about wins. Glorifying your success is a celebration. Now, I'm not condoning the idea of throwing a crazy, expensive party every time there's a success. In my case, that would mean a party daily. For real. But it's important to enjoy the moment. Give thanks to God and the people on your squad who make it possible, and think about all the progress you've made while you climb the next mountain—always keep an eye on the next win.

I know I glorify my own success a lot. Haters try to say

I'm annoying. "They" are evil and envious of my wins, but it's funny to me how "they" keep watching my Snapchat and getting angry. "They" say that I repeat myself too much. I don't care if "they" say I repeat myself too much. In fact, let me repeat myself once again, because the people who say I repeat myself too much are the first ones who can tell you about my new deal or when I'm meeting Fan Luv at a video shoot or a sneaker drop. It's these people who might be rolling their eyes who can tell you exactly what city I'll be in at what time and on what date. Now, tell me that's not effective marketing. Fan Luv and "they" know where I am at all times. If I've got a new alert, you know I'll glorify it. Bless up. I'll say it on Snapchat, Instagram, Twitter. I'll even make calls and let people know. It's all a part of the process, and it's all a part of the vision.

The vision is important. Major key: Glorifying your success is all about presentation. My presentation is flawless. We The Best. The key to wins is that you've always got to present them to your fans in a certain way. When I say *fans,* it doesn't have to mean literal fans. It could be the people who've got love for you—your family, friends, people you work with. It might even be your competition— just anyone who's checking for you. You've got to give all these people your best—your fans because they love you, and your enemies so they can feel the heat you're bringing. Marketing yourself beautifully regardless of your audience is a major key because you never know who's watching. It might be a mogul who likes what they see and wants to give you a future deal.

Make each and every success a vibe. Make that weekly announcement a movie so Fan Luv gets hyped and they want to glorify your success, too.

It's why I have my own directors. We make sure to have the most iconic visuals for each alert. I like to work with one person, or with a group of people who have a style, so you know who it is even before you hear anything. I have my own team of artists who design my We The Best clothing and logos, so the quality's always on point. Not only that, everything is seamlessly integrated—the visuals and the sounds. The key here is to have your own unique voice and style. If you're special cloth, make everything around you just as unique and immediately identifiable. But that doesn't mean everybody gotta go out and get a director or a team of artists. It's just about the details. Maybe it's the way your e-mail signature looks, or the type of business card you have, or what your website looks like. It doesn't need to be fancy, expensive, or high-tech. You could be that person who sends a nice handwritten note because it's what represents you. Everyone can have their own iconic type of alert. You've seen me; even my stay-tuned alerts got alerts. You've got to. That's my energy; everything is on brand.

Know your worth, but "they" gotta know your worth, too. To do that you've got to show them your worth. Spell it out for them, just never, ever be shy about your success. Winners don't hide their wins. And you know that. Don't let "they" tell you that you're feeling yourself too hard or being boastful. This is your life that they're trying to control. That's you letting them put you in a box.

When I was the biggest thing on radio in Miami at 99 Jamz, everyone knew who I was. I'm not just saying that. Plus, I was DJing the biggest clubs on their biggest nights at the time. Everybody would come from New York and L.A. because Miami was the spot. You can see the Miami influence in how hot Versace shirts were with everyone at the time. Plus, the weather's always nice. Everyone got to meet me and they loved me and I ripped it down, but some people—"they"—would be like, "You're just a DJ."

I love being a DJ. I love the artistry. I love scratching and vibing with the crowd and feeling with precision what they want to hear and exactly the point at which they want to hear it, but I'm not going to let anyone decide my successes. I choose my success and I glorify my success. I told them I was a DJ, but I also told them I was going to be the CEO of a record company. I stated simply that I was going to own hotels and real estate and restaurants and a clothing line. I would never listen to "they," and I always did my thing. Telling people what you're going to do puts pressure on you to go out and do it. It's almost like setting yourself a public deadline. And the reason you glorify your success is so that you can show them that everything you said you'd do, you did. You put your money where your mouth is—you show and prove.

Then you get to a point where people start getting invested in you. They'll think to themselves, "Wow, Khaled really went and did it. I thought he was crazy, but this crazy dude actually pulled it off." They start getting curious about what you're going to do next. It's like they see the stakes and they feel the drama and that energy. It starts getting suspenseful!

Glorifying your success is like being a DJ. As a DJ you learn how to create energy. You look out at the club or the stadium and you almost got to be a mind reader to know how to move an ever-changing crowd and intensify the excitement. But I always know when I got them. I glorify my success in the same way. Every win is like when that beat drops. And then, when you've got them open and just dying for the next, that is when it's a celebration, for real.

Just look at my track record. My first album was a success, but the first song off my second album? That's the record that changed my life. "We Takin' Over," that was the ultimate in telling "they" that I'd won.

Another thing that happens when you glorify your success is that it means more success. People like to work with winners. It's human nature that I don't want to get on the phone and talk about losing money with my business associates. Nobody does. You want to talk about wins and blessings; you want to share new deals. That positive vibe is contagious. Everyone wants to work with people who are excited about what they're doing. People want to be put in positions to glorify your blessings with you. If you believe that you're the greatest doing it and the work is stellar, other people will believe it, too. The other key to success is timing. Definitely make sure that the wire hits before you talk about it, but also sequence the alerts to ensure that they produce new success. Let me explain: When that Beyoncé Formation tour announcement dropped, you know I made sure everybody knew. It's only after everybody knows that I call a few people who needed a little encouragement to be enthusiastic about our new project. I'm known for legendary collaborations. So when I was working on my album *Major Key*, I knew that when some of these artists heard about Beyoncé and I called them, they were going to say, "Send the instrumental 911," instead of, "Oh, maybe I'll get around to it." Ha. Don't ever play yourself. When they feel the heat, when they know I've got a new announcement every week, they want to be a part of the vision. So that's why I purposefully hold a few calls.

That's what I mean when I say "More success is always the answer." And by *success* I don't just mean money. Sometimes success is doing the work so you can get to the next success. Success can be graduating school to get the job you want or doing a job that's maybe not so glamorous so that you can learn and get the skill set to do the next job. Success is staying healthy. Not playing yourself is also a success. If you can make billions of dollars, that's success, too. No matter what it is, give thanks and glorify it. And when they ask you, "How's business?" always tell them, "Boomin'."

"Make It a Movie"

You know the true secret behind me being able to get
all these incredible artists to collaborate on songs? Do
you know why this artist might have beef with this other
artist, but they'll both collaborate with me? It's because I
don't talk, I show. I make it a movie. Meaning as in, I make
the music a whole exciting world and bring them into it.
If I want a big artist, I don't bore them with words, I show
them.

I get them in a room with some speakers because then
I know I've got 'em. Me, them, music—that's it. Look at
the people I work with: Kanye, Drake, Jay Z, Future, Ross.
It always works. That's my key. I don't want to sit there
with an outline of what's going to happen. These people
have a thousand meetings and a million phone calls;
they don't have time for the pregame—I show action.
That way the inspiration is undeniable. It doesn't matter
who you are, how rich you are, or how big your last hit
was; if you in the business of making something, you're
always looking for what's next. This is true in any creative
industry. You could make music, write stories, produce

movies, or even engineer the next Snapchat; you're always searching.

If I want you on a record, I might play you two other records you ain't on. And they won't be half-finished ideas or any weak shit. It'll be two other incredible tracks that feature huge artists. And then I'll play the record I want you on. And that's it. It's simple. People need to stop talking about what they're going to do and how hot it's going to be. This is not just the music industry, this is every part of life. The people who have a hundred percent chance of failing are the people who never try. The people who just sit around scheming about all the greatness and never actually go out and do it always lose. If you want anyone to be on your team you have to never be scared to show them that you believe in your work. That means you have to do the work. And you have to make sure your work—your movie—is the greatest experience in the world. Don't tell, show. That's when you know you've got 'em.

I'VE BEEN WITH Khaled for fourteen or fifteen years. He was DJing at Privé when I was introduced to him by Fat Joe. Joe called me and said he had this amazing person that he wanted me to meet and so we went to see Khaled DJ at what was at the time the hottest club in Miami. I'm from New York so this was a type of energy I hadn't seen before—in New York there's kind of a more reserved, chic, understated vibe. Miami is very different and Khaled parties are even more unique. I'd never seen that kind of interaction with the crowd; he was just playing music but just talking to the crowd at the same time and keeping the energy so hyped.

I don't even think we had a formal conversation about how we'd be working together, it was just that since Joe introduced us we were family. Khaled's always had a good sense of style. He is very particular and always had an idea of what he wanted to look like. Our first big job together was the "We Takin' Over" video shoot. He wanted to look very Miami and he wanted the best. I knew it was a big deal because this was how he'd be seen on a global scale as an artist, so it was a challenge. I wanted to do something different from what I was doing with Joe and I wanted him to stand out from Ross, so we developed a style between the both of us.

With each album we'd go to a new level of luxury. It was an evolution from DJ Khaled to an artist and then of course he also had to be seen as a label executive and a mogul. So we incorporated more dress shirts—clean, tailored silhouettes. And when he was comfortable we started to taper and tailor the clothing, which was interesting to him because he historically wore a lot of baggy ensembles. The other thing is since Khaled's parents are in fine men's tailoring and he grew up in fashion he always had an eye for quality fabrics. So he's very discerning in what he likes. He's a man of great quality. He loves silks, Egyptian cottons, he loves cashmere, butter-soft leathers, he loves Loro Piana. If you think about it, his tastes are very Miami in that there's an almost European influence.

The style kept evolving and then we moved into actual suits. This was right in the middle. He'd been at Def Jam for a minute so it was time. And it's almost like he never turned back from that. He's so diverse in his style. He's comfortable in either basketball shorts or a full suit. Khaled and I at this point make a lot of custom pieces together. Like bespoke one-of-one. I remember at one point he was shooting a video and he'd been in New York for quite some time and he said, "I want a fur coat for the video." I was wearing a chinchilla and he said, "I like that. I want to do that." So at this point I'm excited because he'd never wanted to do fur before and of course this is Khaled, so he goes, "I want it to be an experience. I want it to touch the floor." And I'm like, "Khaled, that gives us only three days," and he goes, "But I need that. And I need it to be full-length."

And you know how Khaled's voice gets all low when he really wants something and is passionate about it, so I go, "Okay." And so I'm running out the door and he goes, "I want it dragging on the floor!" So I go to the furrier and for me to deliver that coat to him I had to move mountains. He wasn't used to fittings but I was like, "There's no way we're making a full-length custom chinchilla coat without a fitting," so we go, and I'll never forget his face the first time he put it on. He just looked like a kid in a candy store. He was so happy. That's what I mean by he knows what he wants. He knew what it was like to buy a house, a car, jewelry, but this was him dropping a grip on fashion, and so he's really fun as a client when it comes to that. Now we've been working together for so long, it's just family. I was very blessed early in my career to work with great people who allow you to do what you do, and Khaled's just one of those people. Always has been.

—*Terrell Jones, stylist and wardrobe designer*

KHALED IS A workhorse. He's one of the only artists I know who has a hand in every aspect of the business—he creates the record, he negotiates publishing, handles the features, promotes the album—all of it. Even if he hires you to do a job, he's in the trenches with you at every step. That's what it takes to be the best, and it's working for him.

—Kendell "Young Sav" Freeman, president of Maybach Music Group

DON'T DENY THE HEAT

I got a rule that every executive should abide by. Major key: Never deny the heat. What do I mean by *heat*? I mean that combination of special magic that makes a hit. It's that rare energy that is unmistakable and undeniable. No matter where it comes from, if it comes, you'd better take it. Heat is unpredictable, so let me tell you, the source of that heat may surprise you. God might bless a total nobody with heat, so even if you've never heard of the person a day in your life, if they're bringing you a hit, don't sleep. Don't play around thinking you're too big; when it comes, take it.

Recognizing the heat comes naturally to certain people. I'm blessed in that I can always see it. But sometimes you have to remind yourself: Don't fight the love. Don't fight the hits. Fighting it is a waste of time, and usually it's your own ego getting in your way. You've got to smash doors, not build new ones to keep yourself from success, so trust your heart.

Let me tell you about my biggest record. I really didn't know that heat was coming. "All I Do Is Win" is a track that took my career to another level, and it was the last song I recorded for my record *Victory*. It was the eleventh hour. I was in the studio and literally had to turn the album in in two days. T-Pain and I were working together and he's one of those geniuses who are great to try things out with. He can just show up, go into the booth, and just record in the clutch because he doesn't need anything. We're great friends so we know each other's vibe, and I told him, "Yo, let's win, man." With that, he goes in and goes, "All I do is win, win, win . . ."

He's rare when it comes to melodies. Watching him work will astound you. He writes these hooks so fast and perfect, and we just talk the record up, and then, depending on the day, the heat comes. That night when he went into the booth, literally after everything he did he would look at me and I would have to give him the thumbs-up because it was fire. After he sang the rest of the hook, that part where he goes, "Everybody hands go up!" that's when I said to myself, "Oh my God, we got one."

Mind you, I don't even know what time it is; I know I have two days to finish my album and that what I'm supposed to be doing is mixing and basically putting finishing touches on the records that I have. But I knew that a pathway had opened itself to us and we had to see it through. I know that of course nobody would front on a T-Pain hit. Nobody would deny any heat coming from this man. But the reason I'm including this story in this key is that I had this album all mapped out. This heat had come at an inopportune time. This heat complicated my life by a lot but when it comes, you go.

I remember the moment so vividly. I can hear my heart beating in my ears, I'm sleep-deprived but my mind is going a mile a minute, all I'm thinking is, "This is gonna play in NBA championships." And you know in Florida marching bands are big, so I'm also thinking this is going to be huge with marching bands, and I can hear it all and visualize it and at this point I haven't even put any rappers on it yet. I've just got this hook and no time. I've already told you that Ross lives down the street, so I call Ross and I'm just like, "Yo, Ross, I need you on this record right now. I need you in the room." So Ross comes and he hears it, he knows what it is, so he's rapping, and then I'm like, "Boom."

Then I call Ludacris, like, "Ludacrissssss, I'm telling you. I AM TELLING YOU. This is huge." I'm like, "Check your e-mail. I'm sending you this record right now." He gets it and boom. He comes back quick, like, dahdahdah-dahdah, the way he raps all fast and in the pocket, and I'm just like, "Wow."

And then there was Snoop. Okay, here's the thing with Snoop. Every time I see this man, it just makes me happy, I get excited. Come on, that's Snoop *Dogg*—that's special cloth. So when I see him, I'm like, "I've always wanted to work with you." Because who doesn't want to work with Snoop Dogg? And every time he responds like, "Nephew, let's do it. Let's make it happen. Anytime." People always talk about "let's build," and how they're going to make music together, but this is Snoop. I had every intention of following through on that one. But because he's an icon, that implies a certain amount of pressure. I had opportunities to send him records before, but I knew if I was going to put him on a track it had to be a smash.

Now, remember, I've still only got something like forty-eight hours to deliver my album, the dates are all set and the machine is moving, but the heat came for me. I send Snoop "All I Do Is Win." He sends me back that verse so fast it's unbelievable. That's what I mean by "You can't deny heat." Heat is inspiring. Heat will motivate anybody—it doesn't matter what time it is or how legendary you are. A hit will wake your ass up. I've experienced it, for real.

That record came out, and that's when I knew what it felt like to never have to call anybody to ask them to play something of mine. There wasn't a single DJ I had to browbeat or convince. There were no doors to smash; I didn't even have to lift my hand to open the door. You can't stop hits. And if the people love it, they'll make it big, and man, this record was huge. Not only that, but when we shot the video for the remix over Memorial Day weekend, it was a movie. Everybody came out: Jadakiss, Puff, Nicki Minaj, everyone. We performed at Mansion and ended up doing that song three times back to back, and it felt so good, and I was so grateful. You never know when these triple-platinum blessings will come.

But heat isn't all about music, or even pop culture. Heat is just that raw inspiration. The real key is that the next amazing idea could come at any time, but it can also come from anywhere. Don't be narrow-minded because it's never been done before or because the person who had the idea is the last person you'd expect to come with the greatness. Don't be an instrument of "they" behavior. If it's heat, open the door. Help them smash the next door down and share the win. See that idea through to fruition and make it epic. The magic is bigger than us, and God is mysterious. When he blesses a man or woman with a moment of brilliance, who are you to deny it? These are all opportunities. Matter fact, some of the best opportunities come when you least expect it. And if you've got the ear or the eye or the instincts to see heat even before it really catches fire, meaning as in, before the rest of the world catches up, then you've got to play a part. It's always better to be a pioneer than to jump on some bandwagon. It's called We The Best, not We The Last. When "All I Do Is Win" came, I had a blueprint. I understand deadlines because I'm a businessman and a label owner. I had plans for when I wanted to be done, but sometimes plans change. Heat changes timelines. Heat sometimes alters whole blueprints, maps, and charts. When heat comes, a lot of times everything that came before it ceases to matter. It's moments like these that can move mountains and change a culture. Heat makes history.

"All I Do Is Win" is stadium music. It's timeless. Not to mention my kids' kids are gonna go to college on that record. I constantly think about how that song happened and it's made me more watchful.

Sometimes I'll just sit in the studio, because who knows? Somebody might walk down the hallway and inspiration may strike. You hear about this all the time. An artist walks down the hall, somebody knows someone else, they give each other a pound, they hear something, they get inspired, they record a record, and boom—the record goes triple platinum. That's why I love the game; you could have a thousand wins, but you just never know where the next will hit. It's exciting and you have to respect that the process is unpredictable. You wait for magic. Magic doesn't wait for you.

We work hard every day to try to make that Super Bowl music, and that heat came for me at the last possible minute. If I experience that a few times in my lifetime, I'm blessed. I think it's what we all want—being in that zone—no matter where we live and no matter what we do for work. I get at least ten or twenty requests every three or four days to license that song, and you know me—I approve everything. I know some artists are like, "I don't know about this look or that look," but I'm just like, "Approve everything!" Are you crazy? Let that go off. Make it a movement. My lawyer will be like, "You don't want to read this movie script?" Nah, just put it in the movie. Let them all have the heat. Nobody can deny the heat.

"Success Is a Process"

Several years ago I started getting bad anxiety. And if there's one thing I've learned over the years, it's that for me, managing stress through exercise makes a huge difference. The young world needs to know that everything is a journey—success is a process that turns into progress. Right now I'm trying to lose weight to meet my next goal, which is to fly again. Whenever I go on tour, I have to get on my tour bus. It's a way more expensive mode of getting around, and if Fan Luv sees me in L.A., it means I've been on a bus for days getting to you from Miami. I used to fly but stopped around seven, eight years ago because of the anxiety. I hated all that turbulence, especially on some of these smaller planes, and I'd get panic attacks. The last time I was on a plane, the shaking was so bad that I decided then and there that it wasn't worth it. But you've seen me going hard. I've been blessed with so many opportunities, and I'm thankful to all the people who have helped me, like my trainer and chef, but I'm still working on it. Now, I know not everybody has a personal chef or can work out with famous trainers, but even the most expensive fitness and diet team can't do the work for you. Meaning as in, the hard part you have to do for yourself. Even if it's just a little each day. Even if it's just going for a run around the neighborhood or making sure you bring a healthy lunch to the office. Every day I'm getting closer to my goals, and soon I'm gonna fly around the world. There's so much Fan Luv overseas that I want to meet. I want to hear *Fan Luv* in every language there is, and besides, as amazing as the We The Best tour bus is, you know the We The Best private jet is going to be major.

EVER SINCE THE beginning Khaled has always celebrated positivity, success, and passion. In an era of "gotcha journalism" and all the negativity that comes with the TMZ attitude, it's refreshing. Lately the pendulum has swung hard in the direction of animosity and drama but Khaled ignores all of it.

We're both in the business of positivity and we believe that contributing to the culture is important. And a major key to my success is "Sign stars, don't dust bums off." We're in an industry of ego. You have a lot of people—executives, managers, whoever—who believe that through their influence they can create stars. You don't create stars. Our job is to find stars and get out of their way. You don't sign a bum and dust them off and polish them and hope for the best. That never works. That's not how to shape a future. Khaled and I are in the business of finding stars and guiding them. It's why we win and stay winning.

—*Lyor Cohen, CEO of 300 Entertainment*
and hip-hop pioneer

DON'T CHASE THE MONEY; LET THE MONEY CHASE YOU

Money complicates everything. It's true what Big said. And it can be a setback when you're just out here trying to be a visionary. But let me tell you about what needs to happen once you have food on the table and a roof over your head: Stop chasing money.

It sounds crazy when I say it because we all want money. You might even be like, "Hold up, Khaled, that's easy for you to say because you have money." Of course having money is better than not having it. We all want success. But when I tell you to secure the bag I'm not just talking about the wire. The key is not to chase the money—let the money chase you. Money is confusing. It's easy to chase money because it's natural and that's what most people do. But you're special cloth. If you want not only success but *more* success, you've got to chase the vision. That's the real goal.

I talk about wanting to be a billionaire. I talk about how I want you to call me Billi, but the money isn't the game plan. Money is not the destination of the pathway of more success. The goals are to make only the best, get even better, take shit over, and achieve joy. There are new challenges and successes, and I have to figure out a new business every day. I know that the billion will come.

Here's an example: I know I want to work with Denzel Washington one day. I don't get confused thinking about how much money I'm going to make when I eventually collaborate with Denzel Washington. I keep my mind trained on working with Denzel Washington. That's what I mean by "Chase the vision, not the paper." When I think about my goals for the next year, I don't rank them in order of what's going to make me the most money. I think about what's going to make me happy and what's going to lead to the next opportunity that will make me happy. Put the vision first; that way you're always excited about the wins and what's coming next. They never said winning was easy, but this way you love the work while you're hustling. This way you love the journey—the progress and the process—as much as the result. Major key.

I used to chase money all the time. When you start out, you've got to. But let me tell you what happened once I started being clear to myself and my team about the big picture of what I wanted. We sat down and discussed the next four or five huge moves and how they fit with the vision, and after that my ideas started to pop. When it pops, that money chases you. Believe me. That's how your vision comes to light. It takes a lot of patience and a lot of focus, but once it happens, the blessings are endless.

Let your team know what the goal is and make sure you choose a team that believes in what you believe in. When you do this, the new opportunities will make sense for not only who you are but what your team represents. We The Best. That's not easy to maintain, and we have to be selective. Your team will know what opportunities to present to you. This saves a lot of time. My team, who work with me every day, might have twenty conversations with people wanting to go into business with us. But instead of bringing me a hundred ideas, they'll bring me the ten best. Not the ten most profitable, but the ten best, as we define it. They know what the vision is; we've been working together for years. And when you're working on a bigger picture that everybody believes in, that passion and dedication will show in the work. If that happens, of course the money will chase you; you're making the best.

I wake up with a clear conscience, excited about what the day's going to bring. I am a fan of what I do, and that's a blessing. I'm busy every day, and some days get hectic—believe me—but no matter what the new deals are, I'm passionate. I meet people who inspire me, and I know I inspire them, and it's beautiful. One of my favorite things is to visit the young world at school and talk to them about following their dreams. I love that I can stand in front of them—without reservation—and tell them how happy and successful it made me to follow mine. It feels good not to be a hypocrite.

But what if you don't know your vision? Any moment you ask yourself this question is a perfect time to start thinking about it, no matter if you're young or old. Don't be so impatient trying to prioritize money that you don't ever ask yourself the right questions. For example, who do you look up to, and what jobs do they have? What do you love doing in your free time? Is there a common interest that brought you and your friends closer together? Do you have any passions that you think about a lot but would never dream of attempting? Ask yourself these questions all the time, and don't ignore the answers just because you think they're stupid or implausible. My first passion was breakdancing, and that led to DJing, but it was all a part of my love for hip-hop. I didn't let anybody tell me that hip-hop wouldn't lead to a career or that DJing was just a hobby. Watch out for that word, *hobby*. People love gaslighting you into thinking your career is nothing more than a hobby—a distraction. Don't get discouraged. Turn your interests into a career you can dedicate yourself to. It's exactly what I did and look where I'm at.

Feeding those doubts is a waste of energy, and even worse, you might end up on a journey filled with hate and envy because you're denying yourself joy.

If you have a passion, make that your vision. That sounds simple. Sometimes it can be confusing because it sounds *too* simple. You can find so many reasons not to follow your dreams. It could be that your dream is overwhelming. Sometimes it feels far too risky to admit to yourself that you can make a side hustle into a career or a business opportunity. What if you fail? What if you don't love your dreams anymore *because* you fail? What if making your passion into your career sucks all the fun out of it? What if you're not good at your passion? These are all understandable reservations, but they're all excuses. Of course there will be storms and obviously you won't be good when you're starting out, and there will be failures.

It's a lot easier to stay where you are and wonder what might have been. It's more financially responsible. That's why following money can be a trap. It makes following your dreams seem foolish or wasteful. A single-minded focus on money can make you think that your vision is hurting your future instead of building it. The mind can be very persuasive when you're trying to talk yourself out of something.

It might also be that your passion is in a very competitive industry. Or maybe your vision has never even existed before. I know what this is like—show me another Palestinian mogul who succeeded in hip-hop. The thing is, sometimes you've got to invent who you want to be. This is what I mean when I say you have to rip the doors down.

Chase the dream and create the new blueprint. If there are nobody's footsteps you can follow, create your own and let yours be the ones that the people who come behind you can follow. Then name your own price for this unbelievably unique work you do. It's called being a trailblazer. Let me put it like this: If one path has more money but the other path makes you happier, choose the other path. As long as that path leads to good work. Money is temptation, of course, but money can come with a lot of strings. Don't chase money, and definitely don't chase easy money if it requires a path you don't believe in. You always want to glorify your new deals; you don't want to be embarrassed by them.

Over the years I've had many opportunities to go into fashion. There are so many companies out there that just make T-shirts and slap your name on the front. It's not complicated, but I knew I wanted the best. Besides, with my parents in the garment industry I know quality when I see it. I was raised to see it. I couldn't imagine a situation where I'd put *We The Best* on a product that wasn't the best. Don't ever play yourself. I knew that while I could take that quick check and let another company have my name, the potential for my reputation suffering as a result was high. I don't ever want Fan Luv to be disappointed after ordering something from us. That's not what my relationship with Fan Luv is about. It's about mutual respect and I'm not going to do anything to jeopardize that.

You see me all the time wearing my own T-shirts, flip-flops, and socks. I'll even get custom flip-flops for people on my team and they'll wear them. They'll wear them because they're fly and comfortable and because they're phenomenal quality. If it was just about the money, I could have gone with anyone years ago with little issue. Instead I waited for the right time to make the We The

Best store and to grow my business according to my vision. Of course the money follows.

The thing about chasing the vision is that not everyone can see your vision. It's your dream; it's personal. Meanwhile, everybody can see money; it's universal. A fool with no imagination understands money, and that's why you've got to be strong and have a lot of integrity when following your path.

Your family might not even understand at first. That's natural. Even the closest people to you might not get it. That's okay. Don't be frustrated, because if you just climb the mountain and make good decisions, over time they'll trust you. And if they don't, that's on them. Just don't stop or wait around for people to understand what you're doing. Move on. I told you being special cloth is lonely sometimes, but that's okay. Because being at the top is never lonely. Everybody wants to be around you then. That's when everyone tries to say they saw your vision this whole time, too.

"Patience Is a Talent"

Man, patience really is a talent. Sometimes when you see your vision so clearly, it's challenging not to just want to rush to the next win. I always say timing is everything, meaning as in, there's a right time for everything, so patience is important. My patience has been tested at every step of the way to see the level of success I've seen, and I know in my heart that really big wins take years. But patience has never been a quality that comes naturally to me.

Thing is, sometimes you also have to teach patience to the people around you so they can take time to think. It's everybody's natural inclination to be impatient but when it comes down to making a decision, you don't want to feel stressed. You also don't want to make calls when you're angry or weak. Your business partners might try to force you to choose an option when you're distracted. And it won't be because they're a "they" but because when deals are on the table everything always feels like an emergency. Everyone wants to move on to that next win. Just don't allow someone's impatience to infect you with impatience.

If you can't make a decision at the time, make it tomorrow. Make it three days from now. Tell everybody you've got love for them but you don't want to make an error in judgment that all parties will grow to regret. It might feel like you're letting everyone down or inconveniencing them because they're all waiting on you, but take your time and just be honest. This all sounds obvious, but there are times, especially when the choices get bigger, that you really feel the pressure. Just remember that a good decision is a win for everybody and that you can't always go back on a bad decision. It's called being true to your word. Be patient now or deal with regrets later.

KHALED'S BEEN THE *same swagged-out, determined guy since the first day we met in 1998 when I started Poe Boy. He's got an energetic vibe and we've been through a lot together in this game. For as far back as I can remember I've always had Khaled's back and he's had mine. We both stay humble and feed off of each other's energy whether it's music, marketing, restaurants, or real estate. We broke Rick Ross together and Khaled's always supported my vision, so for that I'm always going to be loyal and trill. When I told him Ross was next he believed and never turned back. Same with Flo Rida. Plus, Khaled never asks for nothing in return. I see him running one of the majors soon. He's earned everything he has today and no one deserves it more. I know we'll continue to win together because our hearts are pure and it's God's plan.*

—E-Class, CEO of Poe Boy Music Group

GOD IS THE GREATEST

Everybody has their own beliefs, but I believe in God. You might not believe in my God, but I hope everybody believes in something. Every second, every breath, every morning, and every night I give thanks. Every chance, even if I don't put my hands to the sky, I'm praying. That's what I mean when I say "Bless up."

There are different names for God, but whether it's Allah, God, Buddha, or whatever other higher power you recognize, God is God. I'm Palestinian. My God is Allah—that's my God. People ask me how I feel about the treatment of Muslims in this country, and I believe you've got to forgive the ignorance. I'm Muslim, and to me it's so important to walk with God and have a relationship with Him. Especially when you're down; that's when you really need Him. When times were tough, I never ever doubted Him. Never. And every time I got down, I got back up. Every time I went broke, I secured the bag. When things got hard I prayed for guidance, and God helped me every step of the way. Taking the time to think about any situation and praying about it helps me see it from a different perspective. Especially if I'm emotional or it's challenging to think clearly.

Early one morning I was on the tour bus, going from Miami to Atlanta, and someone from my management showed me a YouTube link. It was of a reverend in New York at First Baptist Ministry in Queens who gave a sermon to his church for Youth Day. He was wearing a We The Best T-shirt, and he had a great, powerful voice. The minister started off by making some jokes about how he didn't know who I was but Fan Luv in his congregation directed him toward my videos.

The reverend watched those videos and made an unexpected connection. He realized that a lot of what I talk about, a lot of the major keys, is about God. Then he got real inspired and gave an amazing sermon, which inspired me right back.

Now, I know his God might be different from my God, but we both agree that there's power and comfort in believing in something bigger than yourself. That's what I mean when I say the keys are real life—they're universal. It doesn't matter what you believe in, what you do for your job, or where you come from. You can apply the keys to your own situation, regardless of your circumstance. I really have faith in everything that I talk about. I'm no preacher, but I believe my messages because I believe in God, and God is great.

Life can be difficult when you're a boss. There are a thousand decisions a day, and so many people who rely on your judgment, and even more people counting on your money and continued success. You have to set an example, and you feel like you don't ever get a day off and you're never allowed to feel down. I accept this. Life as a boss often feels like no one has your back. But this is why

I have a relationship with God. No matter how big a boss I get to be, man is man and God is God and God will always look out for me.

This is a reassuring thought, so I make sure to remember this at all times. This is why I pray as often as I do. Each time I pray I thank Him for having my back and for making sure that I'm never alone when I make any big decision. But it's not only important to know God if you're a boss. Everybody feels alone. It doesn't matter if you have a big family or have your best friends around you at all times; there will always be those moments when you feel like no one understands you or can help you.

This is the time to talk to your God.

Sometimes "they" might give you a hard time for believing in God. Or "they" might want to argue about which God is the right God. "They" are the ones starting wars in the name of their God and inciting hate and doubt in whatever you believe in. Stay away from "they." Why would anyone try to ruin something that comforts you or gives you power? This is another moment where you have to be yourself. Hold what you personally believe close to your heart and do what works for you. Be thankful for the air you breathe and the new opportunities you have each day. God protects me and my family every day of my life. All day. Thank God for life.

Angels

I call my flowers angels because they're a blessing. I'm grateful to them; I thank God for them. My angels make my musical garden beautiful. My angels, the ocean, Lion, my fire pit, my hammock, my pool—all of this is my paradise. I love being home in Miami, it's my favorite place in the world, and I pray every day because God is great.

You got to protect your paradise. I worked twenty years to have all of this, and I know it's a privilege for me to be home with my angels. You all know that vibes are important to me. Vibes influence energy.

Some nights, when I'm home after a beautiful day and I've been all over the ocean on my Jet Ski and swum in the saltwater, I just look at my angels. You need to have beautiful things around you all the time to remind you that the existence of "they" is balanced out. I work hard every day but life is a blessing, and over the last two years I've had to remind myself to take a moment and enjoy some of the things I've worked hard for. It's about gratitude. Be grateful for your blessings and really take the time to smell the flowers.

I water my angels, and I get to see them grow, and when the sun is up and I take care of them I can see how happy they are. I can also see when the angels are sad. Maybe they're sad because they have to weather a storm, but once it passes my angels are thriving again. My angels are incredible; they signify the best of life.

My grass used to be brown, and now it's green. There's so much evidence in the world that good work makes a difference. I didn't give up. I kept watering and showing my yard love and now everything is abundant and lush. Now my angels show me love. So does my bamboo. Those Mother Nature vibes are important. You've got to take care of everything that shows you these vibes because you know what they say about Mother Nature: Respect your mother.

I MET KHALED when I was working at a label as an A&R in New York about ten years ago. There was a song that his producers, The Runners, had made and I loved it and had my heart set on it. Come to find out it wasn't available and that's when I learned how similar Khaled and I are—I wouldn't let it go. I woke up every single morning at 9 a.m. and it was the first call I made for three months straight. Eventually Khaled called me and was like, "Listen, man. I know you really want this song and I know you've been calling my guys but it's never going to happen. The song's gone, there's nothing I can do."

Then I had Clive Davis call him and give it a shot. No again. So we knew each other throughout the years but we'd never worked with each other beyond this one fiery, slightly contentious encounter over this song that I loved so much. But fast-forward to the last couple of years and we kept running into each other. We did a panel at the Revolt Music Conference together and from there we've always been friendly, but then I had a thought while I was on vacation last December. I picked up the phone spontaneously and said, "Hey, man, I'd love to bring you into the Apple family and do something." He had no idea what I had in mind so I told him the vision from a content and culture perspective. He came to L.A. about three or four times and we decided we were going to work together.

His hustle, passion, doggedness, and just his unwavering faith in his ideas are really inspiring and remarkable. It's not only inspiring, it's contagious. I have that fire within me but when I work with him it drives me in a way that I really like. And he's a fantastic, loyal guy. In fact, he has a heart of gold that sometimes is just too good for the vipers' nest that is the entertainment business. I can't say enough positive things about him.

The thing is, even when you hear things like, "Oh, Khaled won't quit," you have to think that there's a lot of people that you could say that about. But it doesn't mean these people are born equal in this world. Some of us have a unique perspective—our visions are limitless; you could see things in an expansive way that no one else can. Somebody else could work just as hard as Khaled and we all have the same twenty-four hours in the day but it's all about how you use those hours differently from the next guy. Khaled's special. He's a visionary.

—*Larry Jackson, head of content at Apple Music*

I REMEMBER

I might not be the best with names but I always remember a face. I remember what "they" looked like as "they" doubted me, when "they" crossed me, when "they" tried to end me. I also remember how I felt at the time. The rage when "they" laughed at me, or the determination when "they" tried to count me out. I stay away from "they," but I don't forget. Never forget.

Having a long memory is a major key. Some people might call it a gift and a curse, but for me it's only a gift. It helps me remember why I make the choices I make. I told you that I'm grateful for the storm because it makes everything sweeter. It's the same way with remembering those feelings of anger and those faces.

Never underestimate the underdog. I've been the underdog my whole life—being down but never counting myself out. And being the underdog taught me a lot. Following the vision is the goal. But sometimes, when the days get dark, you might momentarily lose your way, say a prayer, and then remember the faces of "they." Use that anger to keep your head up while you weather the storm.

I'm not saying move with hate in your heart—this is not advice for every day. This is for specific moments when you need the extra motivation.

Plus, the key to having good relationships is remembering. It's not about being petty and keeping a catalog of who helped you last and when you helped them. It's not like a banknote or an IOU. It simply helps you keep your word. Just like how some doors take years to break down, certain deals take a while to come together. It's not that you're going back on your word; it's just that timing is key, and it's taking longer than anyone anticipated.

But sometimes just reminding people that you remember is good business. I make hundreds of calls sometimes just to tell people I haven't forgotten them. You've got to be thorough. If I said I would help you with a record or if I told you I would introduce you to someone, I'll do it. It might just take patience on everybody's part depending on what's going on. I go out of my way to remember because I can't even count the number of times people try to avoid me or play themselves waiting for me to forget. But I take my reputation seriously. I don't expect to keep everybody happy all the time, but I do expect to always do everything in good faith.

I also always remember where I come from. Florida raised me. I love Miami; that's my home, and no matter where my work takes me, I will always wave the flag for Miami. It's important to let your sense of identity ground you. It keeps you coming home to people who love you and know you for real. People always try to say, "You changed," like it's a bad thing. I think change is great; change is growth—evolution. But always remember who your family is and where you came from. Miami, for me, is that. It's my guiding light and my perspective.

Florida's changed a lot in my lifetime. I remember when I came out with "I'm So Hood." Ross, Trick Daddy, T-Pain, and Plies were all on the song—and we're all from Florida, so that was such a moment for us. I love hip-hop like I love my home, and there was a long time where hip-hop wasn't represented on the radio in Florida, let alone had serious artists coming from there, so you can only imagine how that made me feel. It feels good to accomplish what "they" told me I was incapable of. My memory has a lot of moments I have to be grateful for. I will always be grateful that Budafuco gave me that first little set at the club. I had to turn that no into a yes, but it kicked off everything. Also, shout-out to Daddy Saw.

I will never forget the people who helped me.

And of course I will always remember Luke. He gave me an opportunity at 99 Jamz, and I will always be honored that he chose me to represent the city. Uncle Luke is special and I salute him. We made history together at that station for real.

I appreciate everyone who ever did anything for me or helped me open any doors. Joey Crack and Pun blessed me. They'd call in to all my radio shows all the time and perform at parties. They showed love. L.A. Reid; Jay Z; Cess Silvera, who directed *Shottas*—all these people saw my strengths and believed in me at a time when not everybody did. I appreciate Kanye West for coming and not only doing "Grammy Family" on my first album, but also doing my video right when he was huge. I appreciate all these people. My life would be darker without them.

That's the thing: The flip side of being able to remember all the "they" faces is that I always also remember the people who showed love. Let me tell you, I got a lot of calls after I became known for the keys on Snapchat, but many of them were from people who rode with me for a long time. Like L.A. Reid, who saw my potential early, or Jay Z and Roc Nation. Not a lot of people know this, but ten years ago Jay Z hit me and offered me a deal before Roc Nation was even announced. This was before he had the sports deals and the tour deals, before they moved into the building on Broadway, before anything. He asked me, and I said, "Jigga, of course." It's Jigga!

But that was my Def Jam year, and it was his early

vision—he hadn't opened the business yet—and the logistics didn't work out. But I knew it was going to be big. It was so meaningful for Jay Z to tell me ten years ago, before all of this, that he wanted to represent me. So when that call came this time and the timing was perfect, it was such a blessing. I really still can't believe it sometimes that Jay Z is my manager.

It's those people whose calls you take first. I know in my example, I'm talking about Jay Z, and who wouldn't take a call from Jay Z—don't ever play yourself—but the key is important for everyone. Always remember who was there for you when you were the underdog. But remember them again when you're on top. It's a long road, and you'll need people you trust on the way. But it's also about the people who saw your vision early. These are the people to never forget. You can trust these people and their taste. These are the people who not only know success when they see it but can detect success before it happens. You want to be on their team, and you want them on yours.

"I Changed . . . a Lot"

When you get a little bit of success, people will try to front on you and tell you that you've changed. They'll say it in this tone, as if it's a negative thing. They might say that you went Hollywood or that you think you're a big shot or this and that, but the point is they say it like you used to be better way back when. That's "they" talk. Of course "they" always want you to stay exactly where you were when you started out. It makes them more comfortable to think that you've stayed on the same level as "they" find themselves on. It's why now when people come up to me and say I changed, I just tell them I changed . . . *a lot*. Because I did. I changed enough to know I don't need their kind of negativity in my life. After I tell them "a lot," I also usually leave. You should, too. I feel bad for people who stay the same. It must get boring.

THIRTEEN YEARS AGO, while on break from my graduate studies at Fordham University, a young man approached a mutual friend asking for my number. A day later I get a message from a "DJ Khaled" asking for a return call. Initially I only knew of "DJ Khaled" as the chief rocker of the best party in Miami that New Yorkers would fly down to hear DJ, otherwise I did not know him. So upon returning the call I wasn't sure of the motive.

"Hi, Khaled, this is Nicole. You left me a message."

"Oh yeah, hey, what's up? You wanna hang out? I'm not working tonight, but you and your girlfriend come hang. I'll pick you guys up."

"Okay, see you later."

To my surprise a very energetic, determined young DJ/radio personality with the ambition, mind-set, and spirit of an aspiring mogul picks me up with one of his friends to vibe for the night. Well, let me tell you, *determined* doesn't even give justice to the word. Within a year I was coerced and convinced to give up my dreams and relocate from New York City to Florida. From day one he would tell me "You're my wife"— I'm thinking he's crazy—but this man, my friend, my lover, my brother, my uncle, my side, front, and back is the most driven, hard-working, adamant man that I've ever met and ever will.

I am proud to say that through all of the struggles in life, from being a DJ to an aspiring producer to an executive producer; from the mixtapes to the singles to the number one albums; from the agonizing plane rides to the local shows on tour buses to the national tours; from the little dirty hotels on the road to the mansions; we are here, together and stronger than ever! You have accomplished your goals when everybody laughed and said that we were crazy, but we always had each other to believe in. From the notes on the fridge every Christmas with the New Year's aspirations to knocking them out every year and starting new ones! I am happy that I believed in the young crying cub that became the roaring lion. And as far as I can see, the journey has just begun! With all of my love and support, always and forever!! WE THE BEST!!

—*Nicole Tuck, spiritual advisor and life partner*

WIN, WIN, WIN, NO MATTER WHAT

All my life I've had to rip down doors, break out of boxes, fight for what's mine, never surrender, and that's never going to stop. I expect storms and never get comfortable with the wins, and that's how I stay winning. But, man, let me tell you, these days, when I look around me and truly reflect on this past year, I have to give thanks because it's been so exceptional. The blessings on blessings surprise even me. Right now I have the number one album in the country. It took ten years and I've had a lot of wins, but *Major Key* is so special to me. And it means so much to me that I get to announce such a blessing in this book to you, Fan Luv. Plus, I want to take the time right here to celebrate what I already know will be the number one book because I'm going to speak it into existence, and

I hope that you enjoy my blood, sweat, and tears in these pages. I pray that you're inspired by my stories.

I keep pinching myself when I think about this year. I've been to the White House. Twice. I've sat at a table with the president of the United States to talk about what we can all do to make the future brighter for our kids. I was even invited to the White House Correspondents' Dinner. That's crazy. And this was all going down while I was invited on the Formation tour with Beyoncé. Plus, you've seen the logos. Apple, Epic, Roc Nation.

But it doesn't matter if I become a household name, or what phone calls I get, or what wire hits. Every time I put a win on the board, I turn to my team and I tell them, "Let's win more." Don't misunderstand me. It's not about ego and it's not about being greedy. I don't achieve more so that I can compete with another mogul. It's not about money or how many mansions I could have. It's not about the Jet Skis, the shoes, the watches—it's not about any of that. I told you, don't chase the money, the money will chase you. For me the greatest part of the reward is just getting to do what I do. It's that simple.

The biggest success is the honor of doing the work that you love. But the only way you're guaranteed to stay being able to do what you do is if you're successful. That's why I say win, win, win, no matter what. And not only that, but the answer is always more success. Going hard can never stop. Winning can never stop. I'm not trying to be an industry secret. I don't want to be the independent dude everyone loves. I want to go big and be number one in everything I do. I want to share my keys with everybody, no matter where you are or what you do, because I really believe they will help you.

We The Best is about staying the best. Raise the bar. Keep moving the goals, and keep hitting them. Then, surpass them.

You've got to stay hungry. Just because I have the number one album doesn't mean I'm not thinking about the next goal. You have to wake up each day with that fire, that same energy you had on day one. You have to stay motivated. Getting comfortable is dinosaur shit. Not watching your back for what's next will guarantee your extinction. And don't ever think you're too big to fail. Ego-fueled behavior like that will end you. It's that simple.

Listen carefully: Success breeds more success. People love you when you're hot. I tell you people kick you when you're down and want to kick it with you when you're up. But it's not just them. Everybody loves winners. It doesn't matter what culture you come from or what country you're from. People understand when you shine. Everybody—even "they"—recognizes success when they see it. Plus, winners attract winners. When successful people do business together, the investments just come. I talk about another one. *And another one.* It's because each success is an opportunity for the next success. If you can't make that connection, and if you don't keep working for that connection, you're over. Never surrender.

Always secure your bag and stay focused, but the second that wire hits is when you need to be thinking about the next win, and the win that comes after that. Always stay three moves ahead, and cook with everything you've got. Keep as many deals and projects going as long as you can without the quality of the work suffering. Know your limits, but never forget that sometimes when the time is right, you have to push past them.

People don't tell you this, but after a while it might seem like the uphill battle isn't a battle anymore. It might appear at times that people are opening doors for you and inviting you in. It's a beautiful feeling to be standing there ready to throw everything you've got at the door, only to find out that you don't have to lift a finger. But the day every battle feels relaxed you'd better wake up. That means you retired and you didn't even know it. If you don't feel challenged at all, you need to look around and see if you ain't missing opportunities that you should be up on. You need to be thinking about why you're not setting your sights on the next level of your life. It's important to be curious about new opportunities. Don't ever forget that.

When I think about Snapchat, it's amazing to me that I have fans who don't know about my early music. They might be a little bit younger, and they'll discover major anthems that they didn't even know about. It just shows me that you can't rest on previous accomplishments. People who support you might not know or care what you did a year before, let alone ten years before. That inspires me. That means that I have to constantly work hard to invite new generations of Fan Luv to appreciate me and what I do.

You can't just be successful at one step of the mountain and then chill. You've got to get to the top. And once you get to the top, you've got to keep looking up to see how that next mountain's looking. It's like you can't just be the biggest fish in a tiny-ass pond. You got to swim out to the ocean and do it big. See big things and really understand how much more there is out there. The key is to keep growing. That's what I mean by "The answer is always more success." We have to give thanks for every day, because every day is a step on the pathway of more success. When it comes to progress, every step counts.

"Another One"

Positivity is important—it's great to have an optimistic energy—but it's also helpful to use positivity to fuel your competitive nature. I never graduated high school. People always told me I would never be what I wanted to be. I came from nothing and lived in my car. But if you believe that you can do it, make sure and do it. I'm competitive; I'm confident. I bet on myself and I believe in myself. Plus, I *am* myself. I also choose to be happy no matter what negativity and hate is out there—I stay away from "they."

I have the best management team, the best friends, an amazing family, a flourishing business, and a number one album. I got all these things by following the keys. I told you in the beginning of this book that the keys will help you. I showed you how they applied to a career in entertainment but also how they apply to your job no matter your vision. Plus, I taught you how to use the keys to better your personal life with your friends and your family. You've heard of the keys, but this is a deeper dive into what I mean. I love Fan Luv and with this I want to show you how much.

Now that you've read the keys, go out into the world and win. Do your best. Like I always say, be a star, be a superstar. And then win more. And when your life is filled with so much joy that you feel like your heart will burst, share that joy and teach everyone you love the keys. That's what I mean by another one. And another one. Another one.

Acknowledgments

I want to thank God; my family; my friends; the team; Mary, the writer; and of course Fan Luv.

ABOUT THE AUTHOR

DJ Khaled is a music-industry mogul, an executive, a megaproducer, and a recording artist who has made dozens of chart-topping records with artists such as Jay Z, Nas, Kanye, Drake, Ross, Lil Wayne, Chris Brown, Ludacris, and more. The founder of We The Best Music Group, he's been signed to such legendary labels as Def Jam, Universal, and Apple. He currently has his group under Epic Records. Khaled is also the creator of one of the most globally viewed social media accounts of the twenty-first century (on Snapchat) with nearly six million followers. He resides in Miami.